Don't Guess

Don't Guess

An Introduction to Objective Tests in English Language

R.A. Banks, MA, Ph.D.

HODDER AND STOUGHTON
LONDON   SYDNEY   AUCKLAND   TORONTO

British Library Cataloguing in Publication Data

Banks, R.A.
   Don't guess: an introduction to objective
   tests in English language.
   1. English language—Composition and exercises
   I. Title
   808'.042'076   PE1413

   ISBN 0-340-36456-4

First published 1985

Set in 11/12 pt Ehrhardt Medium by Macmillan India Ltd.,
157 Brigade Road, Bangalore 560 025.
Printed and bound in Great Britain for
Hodder and Stoughton Educational,
a divison of Hodder and Stoughton Ltd,
Mill Road, Dunton Green, Sevenoaks, Kent
by Page Bros (Norwich) Ltd

For Mary-Lou

Contents

Acknowledgments

For permission to quote copyright material the authors and publishers wish to thank: Chatto & Windus for an adaptation of part of 'The Jungle' from *Living Dangerously* by F Spencer Chapman; Collins Publishers Ltd for 'The Plague' from *The Black Death* by P Ziegler; The Controller of Her Majesty's Stationery Office for an extract from *The Highway Code*; Granada Publishing Ltd for an extract from *The Drunken Forest* by Gerald Durrell; Hamish Hamilton Ltd for an extract from *Vintage Thurber* by James Thurber © 1940 James Thurber, © 1968 Helen Thurber, published by Harper & Row, and for an extract 'Running Away' from *I'm the King of the Castle* by Susan Hill; Hamish Hamilton Ltd and © 1973 The Executors of the Estate of the late L P Hartley for 'A Summons, a Little Sister's Nightmare' from *The Complete Short Stories* by L P Hartley; William Heinemann Ltd and Viking Penguin Inc. for an extract from *The Red Pony* by John Steinbeck © 1933, 1937, 1938 by John Steinbeck, © renewed 1961, 1965, 1966 by John Steinbeck; William Luscombe Publishers Ltd © 1974 for an extract from *Football Classified: An Anthology of Soccer*, edited by Willis Hall, 'Child's Play'; MacDonald & Co (Publishers) Ltd for an extract from *The Dictionary of Puns* by J S Crosbie; Octopus Books Ltd for four extracts from *Strange but True* (ed. Tim Healey, 1983) and two extracts from *The World's Worst Disasters*; Laurence Pollinger Ltd and The Estate of Mrs Frieda Lawrence Ravagli for an extract from *The Phoenix* and for 'The Snake' from *The Complete Poems of D H Lawrence* by D H Lawrence; *Punch* for an anonymous poem; Schools Abroad Ltd for use of *A Taste of France* school travel brochure; Martin Secker & Warburg Ltd for two extracts from *A Separate Peace* by John Knowles; Noel Streatfield for an extract from her work *The Circus is coming*; The Literary Executors of the Estate of H G Wells for 3 extracts from *The History of Mr Polly* by H G Wells; The Times Newspapers Ltd for *The Motor-bike* by Ronald Faux (*The Times* 3.1.81); University of London University Entrance and School Examinations Council for an *English Language Examination*, Paper 2, January 1982; Frederick Warne (Publishers) Ltd for a map from Arthur Banks' *World Atlas of Military History*.

Every effort has been made to trace copyright holders of material reproduced in this book. Any rights not acknowledged here will be acknowledged in subsequent printings if notice is given to the publisher.

Introduction

This is a book about reading closely and accurately. This skill of 'comprehension' is not an easy one to acquire quickly. It requires attention to detail and a sensitivity to the meaning of words used within a context; it rests on the ability to justify an interpretation from what actually exists on the printed page. The aim of this book is to give practice in the careful reading of English so that the skill of 'comprehension' can be developed.

The varied material provided is intended for use in the middle years of the secondary age-range. *Part One* provides some 'fun' exercises in understanding how words build into sense. Letters, words, sentences, and paragraphs are jumbled together and need to be sorted out into patterns of English which convey meaning. Practice in distinguishing what is true from what is false in interpreting meaning follows, and this part of the book concludes with a survey of the forms objective tests can take and a series of 'Do-It-Yourself' exercises in constructing questions. At the heart of all these activities lies the need to read closely, to understand, and to respond to words within a context.

Part Two of the book consists of twenty passages from personal, factual, imaginative, and transactional writing of the kind likely to attract and keep the interest of the Middle-School boy or girl. The questions based on these pages cover the traditional range of objective tests and include true/false, four-option, five-option, direct questions, single-completion, multiple-completion, and *EXCEPT*-type items of the kind set for such pupils later on in 16+, CSE, and GCSE examinations. The passages and the questions become progressively more challenging as the book proceeds and by the time the pupil has learnt the skills implicit in the exercises he or she should be able to go confidently on to the companion volumes more specifically intended for the later stages of 16+ examination preparation (*New Objective Tests in English Language* and *Objective Tests in English Language for GCE* (both by B. Rowe and R. A. Banks and published by Hodder and Stoughton)).

A book which consists largely of passages and objective tests runs some risk of being used in isolation from the rest of the work in the English classroom. I am anxious that this should not happen. Teachers of English are, of course, dealing all the time with careful analysis, the development of response, understanding, and reasoning as well as stimuli to good writing, listening, and talking. The material in this book can, and should, be discussed and integrated with other English activities, and the *Development* sections given at the ends of the sets of questions suggest ways in which this can be done through projects, further reading, discussion and debate, and further writing. The isolation of the study of Comprehension and objective tests can, therefore, be avoided; the passages and the questions can easily be used as springboards into lively and interesting English work.

The book is *not* intended as a series of examination exercises but rather as a source-book of material which, in the hands of an involved and enthusiastic English teacher, can develop the interest of pupils in reading closely and responding sensitively to good writing of the kind they are likely to meet in using and enjoying English. It can also provide some insights into comprehension and practice in objective tests for those working on their own as private students learning English.

Finally, I should like to thank my wife, Mary-Lou, for her encouragement and patience and Mrs Daphne Meeking who, once again, produced an immaculate typescript from a manuscript heavily marked with second, third, fourth and sometimes even *fifth* amendments.

R. A. B.
Sunbury-on-Thames, 1984.

Part One

How to avoid guessing

To misread or to ignore a notice such as this at a level-crossing, where high-speed trains using overhead power lines run, might carry a severe penalty. Normally, careless reading results in far less dramatic punishments; careless reading can cost lives, but it can also leave us out of pocket, misled or confused.

We are not born with the ability to read carefully; we have to work quite hard to become skilled at it. In many examinations candidates fail simply because they have not bothered to acquire this ability.

Part One of this book gives you some puzzles to solve and some interesting passages to read, to think about, and to work out meanings from. You will need to concentrate hard.

Chapter 1

Making Sense of it

In order to understand words, sentences, paragraphs, and the various parts that make up articles and books we have to be able to recognise the following:

(a) the way the components (letters, words, phrases, etc.) are arranged;

(b) the way these components work together and depend on each other.

The exercises which make up this chapter will help you to become more familiar with the way words and sentences are formed and help you to study the way they join together to convey meaning.

Jumbled letters, words and sentences

Exercise 1

In the following sentences, the letters in the words have been jumbled together. Rewrite the sentences correctly.

1. Nac ouy drustanned twah uyo rea ginrade?
2. T'si seay tub ti kates emos gontris tuo.
3. Drows showe telrets rae deblumj hergetto rea lacled marganas.
4. Tub heyt rea garnamas lyon fi heyt kame wen drows.
5. Crowdsross ro braScelb era chum eorm nuf.
6. Temmissoe ouy nac sguse het sword ta ceon.
7. Ta herot semit uyo veha ot krow meth tou.
8. Pelmis decos nac eb dema pu sinug telrets.
9. Sedoc sued yb pessi rae chum erom pactdelicom.
10. Ouy eden ot eb a dogo respell rof hist sexercie.

Exercise 2

In the following sentences, the words are in the wrong order. Rewrite them to make proper sentences.

1. games interesting help of the computers sometimes are played with.
2. an enemy they involve destroying and chasing often.
3. why always so I wonder they violent are!
4. out killer it be the coming must instinct.
5. things want men to destroy all and not women.
6. about games like what the you see would to?
7. dramatic need perhaps bringing those in help not so is to.
8. exciting victims a help to relief earthquake mission could be.
9. time every destruction interception of space and the outer invaders give me from!
10. other athletics game on a computer sport or based not invent some why?

Exercise 3

In the following sentences the letters of the words and the words themselves
are in the wrong order. Rewrite them to make proper sentences. (They are
all the opening sentences of famous stories. Can you recognise any of them?)
1. On pu erwe tereh instacur.
2. nam a dah owt inatcer noss.
3. a erwe ereth nupo sarbe ereth onec-emit.
4. saw dol deshif who eh na nam noela.
5. 12ht xis oklo'cc ym ti saw on diFyard I dan enuJ pu yardthib kewo ta
dernow; no.
6. reha ot terfwis geban dan hwich a stitoreo a fo hemt saw het utpisde.
7. saw intarce thiwe entkit ot ti thiw ginthon eno night hatt het dah od ahd.
8. dah ettase ym mahtingtoNerish afther a ni llams; aws I noss het drith fo
evif.
9. norb het reay I ni 1632 swa, ni orkY hte fo tyic.
10. Hitobbs si thiw ygellar sith nednoccer okob.

Exercise 4

The following contains parts of sentences not in their correct order. Rewrite
the sentences, putting all the parts together in their right order.

e.g. *(a)* and kicked it under the sofa; *(b)* his foot touching a slipper; *(c)* to
see what it was; *(d)* he bent his head down. *His foot touching a slipper, he
bent his head down to see what it was – and kicked it under the sofa.*

1. *(a)* after the flood had dropped; *(b)* to go forth and multiply; *(c)* which
had lasted forty days; *(d)* Noah told all the animals.
2. *(a)* we're sorry but we're adders; *(b)* Noah found two snakes;
(c) because they had to refuse and said; *(d)* who were crying;
(e) clearing up afterwards.
3. *(a)* course I can; *(b)* when the teacher asked the boy; *(c)* and astonished;
d) the pupil replied; *(e)* if he could give Napoleon's nationality; *(f)* the
teacher agreed.
4. *(a)* and as he stood among a herd of dinosaurs; *(b)* don't just stand
there; *(c)* the unsuccessful caveman had returned home empty-handed;
(d) slay something; *(e)* his wife called out.
5. *(a)* no I always talk like this; *(b)* the telephone operator became angry;
(c) have you got the right code; *(d)* and asked; *(e)* but the caller
misunderstood and replied.
6. *(a)* out of a sense of rivalry; *(b)* two friends always bought the same
stamps; *(c)* that imitation is the sincerest form of philately; *(d)* in the
firm belief; *(e)* when they took up stamp-collecting.
7. *(a)* called Carmen Cohen; *(b)* who was called Carmen at home; *(c)* so
that she hardly knew; *(d)* there was a girl; *(e)* and Cohen at school;
(f) whether she was Carmen or Cohen.

8. *(a)* 'Gladiator'; *(b)* it hardly reassured his guests; *(c)* when he said; *(d)* after the cannibal had finished eating; *(e)* as they asked after his mother-in-law.
9. *(a)* that that is is; *(b)* it is; *(c)* is not that so; *(d)* that that is not is not;
10. *(a)* to put bigger spaces; *(b)* between *Dog* and *and*; *(c)* of *The Dog and Manger*; *(d)* the painter was told by the publican; *(e)* when he had finished the sign; *(f)* and *and* and *Manger*.

Exercise 5

The following is a poem about the night bombers which attacked Hitler's Germany during the 1939–1945 World War. The lines are out of order. Rewrite the poem with the lines in their proper places:

Eastward they climb, black shapes against the grey
From English fields. Not theirs the sudden glow
Of falling dusk, gone with the nodding day,
Only to fly through cloud, through storm, through night,
Nor turn until, their dreadful duty done,
Unerring, and to keep their purpose bright
Westward they climb to race the awakened sun
Of triumph that their fighter-brothers know

Exercise 6

The following is a recipe taken from a prehistoric cookery book for dinosaur soup. The steps in the instructions are out of order. Rewrite the recipe by putting the instructions in their proper sequence:

Serves 4000.   Preparation time: three weeks.
Ingredients: one young, tender dinosaur (**not** a brontosaurus);
        50 kg. salt;
        300 gallons of water;
        73 leeks; 56 carrots; 23 turnips.
        acorn wine (optional) – half a bottle.
1. Catch a young animal. (Avoid the angry parents.)
2. Joint the carcass and wash the joints under a waterfall.
3. The acorn wine may now be added, if desired.
4. Kill, skin, and gut the creature.
5. Make a stock with the leeks, salt, and other vegetables.
6. Allow to cool and use as a cold consommé.
7. Remove the meat from the bones and dice it into three-inch cubes. (This is long and tedious but must be done carefully.)
8. Place the dinosaur pieces in the stock and simmer for two-and-a-half weeks.
9. It may be served in wooden helmets used as bowls.
10. Alternatively, it can be reheated as required.

Exercise 7

Look closely at the historical maps given below and then, using most of the information they contain, write a short 'History' composition (of about 200 words) on the importance of the English Channel to Britain in times of war:

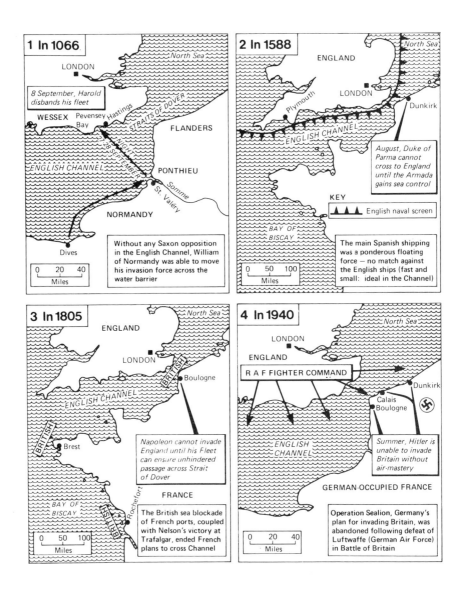

1 In 1066

North Sea

LONDON

8 September, Harold disbands his fleet

WESSEX   Pevensey   Hastings   STRAITS OF DOVER
         Bay

FLANDERS

NIGHT 28TH SEPTEMBER

ENGLISH CHANNEL   PONTHIEU

Somme

St. Valéry

NORMANDY

Dives

0   20   40
    Miles

Without any Saxon opposition in the English Channel, William of Normandy was able to move his invasion force across the water barrier

2 In 1588

North Sea

ENGLAND

LONDON   Dunkirk

Plymouth

ENGLISH CHANNEL

August, Duke of Parma cannot cross to England until the Armada gains sea control

KEY

▲▲▲ English naval screen

BAY OF BISCAY

0   50   100
    Miles

The main Spanish shipping was a ponderous floating force — no match against the English ships (fast and small: ideal in the Channel)

3 In 1805

North Sea

ENGLAND

LONDON

BRITISH   Boulogne

ENGLISH CHANNEL

BRITISH

Brest

Napoleon cannot invade England until his Fleet can ensure unhindered passage across Strait of Dover

BAY OF BISCAY

Rochefort   BRITISH

FRANCE

0   50   100
    Miles

The British sea blockade of French ports, coupled with Nelson's victory at Trafalgar, ended French plans to cross Channel

4 In 1940

North Sea

LONDON

ENGLAND

R A F FIGHTER COMMAND

Dunkirk

Calais
Boulogne   卐

ENGLISH CHANNEL

Summer, Hitler is unable to invade Britain without air-mastery

GERMAN-OCCUPIED FRANCE

0   20   40
    Miles

Operation Sealion, Germany's plan for invading Britain, was abandoned following defeat of Luftwaffe (German Air Force) in Battle of Britain

Jumbled paragraphs

Exercise 8

The following passage is about a father who tried to develop his six-year-old son's growing interest in football. The paragraphs are printed out of order. Re-write the passage with the paragraphs in their proper sequence. (Do not change the order of the material within any single paragraph itself.) Start with the paragraph marked with an arrow (→).

'What's happened to your Liverpool badge?'

'Which ones are Leeds United?'

'Why not?' I tried to keep calm.

To be absolutely honest, my heart rose. I couldn't really fault the lad for I have been a Leeds United supporter all my life.

→ I bought the boy a buttonhole badge and, the very next day, he set off for school displaying it, bravely.

'I'm not Liverpool any longer'

A couple of months ago, I took him to see his first full ninety minutes of football. Not Leeds United, for we live in the South of England, but the local team of which I am club president. We stood on the terraces together, father and son, along with a couple of hundred other stalwarts. The lad watched the game for several minutes and then ventured:

'Oh!'

He came home without it.

'Because Harold Bullock, in my class, says Liverpool are rubbish. Anyway, I'm Leeds United now.'

'Neither. The ones in the blue-and-gold are St Albans, and the ones in the white are Dulwich Hamlet.'

As far as I could gather, the answer neither surprised nor displeased him. Neither did it seem to interest him greatly. Some minutes later he drifted away from the terraces and spent the remainder of the first forty-five minutes throwing Coca-Cola bottle tops at the park railings.

Missing words and idea

Exercise 9

(a) In the following sentences key words important for the sense, have been omitted. Rewrite the sentences choosing the best word(s) from those given in brackets to fill the gaps:

  1. Kangaroos are well-known for their ability to — their young in their pouches. (breed, carry, feed, hibernate, hide)
  2. Leopards are most easily recognised by their — . (fangs, tails, spots, eyes, claws)

3. Those who oppose fox-hunting object most strongly to its —.
(dressing-up, stupidity, class-distinction, cruelty)
4. Those who — fox-hunting argue that it would be wrong to restrict the liberty of the individual. (introduce, ignore, watch, support, tolerate)
5. Many countries have set up — in order to preserve endangered species of animals in their own habitats.
(customs barriers, private zoos, wild-life safaris, nature reserves, local committees)

(b) Read the following passage and then fill in the blanks in the following sentences with an appropriate word:

> The experienced ear of Gabriel Oak knew the sound he now heard to be caused by the running of the flock with great velocity. He jumped out of bed, dressed, tore down the lane through a foggy dawn, and ascended the hill. The two hundred ewes seemed to have absolutely vanished from the hill. There were fifty with their lambs, enclosed at the other end as he had left them, but the rest, forming the bulk of the flock, were nowhere. Gabriel called at the top of his voice the shepherd's call.
> 'Ovey, ovey, ovey!'
> Not a single bleat. He went to the hedge – a gap had been broken through it. A horrible conviction darted through Oak. With a sensation of bodily faintness he advanced. Oak looked over the precipice.

1. Gabriel Oak knew what the sound he heard was because of his —.
2. The noise of the flock running made it clear that they were moving —.
3. The way that Gabriel Oak rushed to the hill suggests that he — the worst.
4. Gabriel Oak at first could offer no — of where the two hundred ewes had gone.
5. Fifty ewes with their lambs were still in their —, where Oak had left them.
6. These fifty ewes and their lambs had formed the — of the original flock.
7. Gabriel Oak shouted — after the missing sheep.
8. 'Ovey, ovey, ovey!' seems to have been a — call used by the shepherds in the area for generations.
9. The sheep normally — to Oak's call by bleating.
10. When he looked over the precipice, Gabriel — to find all his sheep dead.

(c) The following passages contain some gaps in the stories at the points indicated by strings of dots (. . . . .). Try to work out what details of

the stories have been left out by reading carefully what has just gone
before and what happens immediately afterwards:

(i) I hardly knew whether I had slept or not; suddenly I was wide
awake because . . . . . I rose and sat up in bed, listening. There
was nothing. I tried again to sleep but, this time quite
distinctly, ... 'Who is there?' Nothing answered. I was
chilled with fear. Then there was a demoniac laugh. Now I knew
it came from behind the panels . . . . .
I hurried on my frock and shawl and . . . . . . When I got there
the whole of the corridor was full of a strong smell of burning;
smoke rushed in a cloud from Mr. Rochester's room.
Immediately . . . . . . and saw tongues of flame darting round his
bed. The curtains were on fire. Mr Rochester lay stretched so
motionless that it seemed . . . . . .

(ii) One afternoon a big wolf waited in a dark forest for . . . . . .
Finally, a little girl *did* come along and she *was* carrying a basket
of food. 'Are you carrying that basket to your grandmother?'
asked the wolf. The little girl said she was. So the wolf
inquired . . . . .; the little girl told him and then he . . . . . When
she arrived, she opened the door of her grandmother's house. It
was obviously not her grandmother in the bed but the wolf, for
even dressed in a nightcap and gown . . . . . . And so the little girl
took an automatic out of her basket and . . . .
Moral: It is not so easy to fool little girls nowadays as it used to
be.

Exercise 10

Read the following description of the way the German bombing of London
in 1940 and 1941 affected the lives of those living in the town at the time.
    After it, you will find a list of the difficulties Londoners had to face but
they are not in the order they were given in the passage. Rearrange this list to
give the difficulties in their original order in the passage.

Night after night the bombers came but they were picked up by radar
stations mercifully left standing by the Luftwaffe. In addition to the
homelessness the raids caused, however, Londoners had to contend
with more dirt and more broken glass than many of them thought
possible, as they fumbled their way along in the black-out, deafened by
the fearful noise of the sirens (reduced on Churchill's orders from a
two-minute to a one-minute wail). Children ran the severe risk of street
accidents and the numbers of them killed or injured rose sharply.
Those at school in the city suffered in other ways, too. The schools they
attended were occupied by emergency fire-brigades and air-raid
wardens' posts; classes were interrupted or suspended and it was

impossible for them to do their homework in air-raid shelters; and
along with other large public gatherings, football matches between
their favourite local teams were cancelled or postponed.

1. There was a danger of street accidents.
2. Schools were occupied by fire-men and air-raid wardens.
3. The black-out caused problems.
4. Classes were interrupted.
5. Dirt and broken glass were everywhere.
6. The noise of the air-raid sirens was unbearable.
7. Public entertainments were restricted.
8. Homework could not be done.
9. More children were killed or injured on the roads.

Chapter 2

Can you recognise the truth when you see it?

In this chapter you will find some passages which are of various kinds: one describes a performance at a circus, another is part of a story about a pony, a third is an extract giving an account of a very strange trial, another is a factual account of the way reggae started, and the final one describes a spectacular firework display.

Reading to discover the true and the false

Read each of the passages through as carefully as you can. Try to see in detail what its central theme is and the way the writer presents it.

Then turn to the questions that follow. They consist of statements which are either **true** or **false**. Try to decide which are true and which are false by going back to the passage and finding evidence to support what you decide. Write a sentence of your own, preferably by quoting from (or referring back to) the passage wherever possible, to explain why you think each of the statements is true or false.

Begin your own sentence as follows:

I think this statement is true (or false) *because* . . .

DO NOT GUESS. THINK OF A REASON TO BACK UP YOUR DECISION.

Exercise 11

The Circus

If ever a dog knew she was clever that one did. She had no sooner finished her act than she began to show off. She was just like a small child who gets above herself at too much praise. She raced round the ring fence while Lucille tried to catch her. She chewed up a ball. She walked on her hind legs without being asked to. And finally, when   5
Lucille had sent all the dogs away and was bowing in the ring, she came shooting back and bowed too. Lucille was rather fat, with a good deal of her both behind and in front. The dog had evidently noticed this; it made her give rather clumsy bows. You would not think a dog could imitate a fat woman bowing, but this one did.   10

Then into the ring tumbled the clowns. We had seen Gus in various clothes playing various tricks, but this time he came on with a lasso. He caught the other clowns round the neck and then caught himself in the lasso. He skipped with it. He did it beautifully, but he looked so pleased each time he got through the rope safely that you felt it was only by luck   15 he had done it. Finally he lassoed three clowns at once, caught them all, then got his own foot tangled in the end of the rope, and was dragged out of the ring on his back.

1. The comparison between the dog and 'a small child' is intended to show how the dog was trying to draw attention to itself by putting on a display.
(TRUE/FALSE)

2. The words 'gets above herself' (line 3) means 'becomes conceited'.
(TRUE/FALSE)

3. The dog described in lines 1–10 was rather an exhibitionist.
(TRUE/FALSE)

4. Lucille tried to catch the dog as she raced round the ring fence (lines 3–4) because this was obviously not part of the act.
(TRUE/FALSE)

5. The fact that the dog 'chewed up a ball' (line 4) shows that she was not out of control.
(TRUE/FALSE)

6. Lucille was 'bowing in the ring' (line 6) because her act with the dogs had finally ended.
(TRUE/FALSE)

7. The dog's behaviour described in lines 8–10 was intended to suggest that she was rather ill-behaved.
(TRUE/FALSE)

8. The thing that the dog 'had evidently noticed' (line 8) was that Lucille was fat.
(TRUE/FALSE)

9. The woman gave 'rather clumsy bows' (line 9) because she knew the dog was mocking her.
(TRUE/FALSE)

10. The word 'tumbled' (line 11) suggests that the clowns made a noise as they entered the ring.
(TRUE/FALSE)

11. Gus (line 11) was obviously the ringmaster of the circus.
(TRUE/FALSE)

12. The words 'this time' (line 12) make it clear that Gus had not come on with a lasso before.
(TRUE/FALSE)

13. The first trick Gus did with the lasso was to make the other clowns fall over.

(TRUE/FALSE)

14. A lasso is a long rope with a running noose often used by cowboys to catch cattle and horses.

(TRUE/FALSE)

15. The way Gus skipped with the rope shows that he had not rehearsed it very carefully.

(TRUE/FALSE)

16. The word 'beautifully' (line 14) suggests that Gus skipped with the rope very skilfully.

(TRUE/FALSE)

17. The audience felt Gus had got through the rope safely as he skipped (lines 14–15) because he seemed to be happy and surprised each time he managed it.

(TRUE/FALSE)

18. The final act of Gus with the clowns was unfortunately very clumsy.

(TRUE/FALSE)

19. The fact that Gus was 'dragged out of the ring on his back' (lines 17–18) was funny partly because he had in effect lassoed himself.

(TRUE/FALSE)

20. The writer seems to have forgotten, as he described the circus acts, that there was an audience present.

(TRUE/FALSE)

Exercise 12

The New Pony

Jody's father unhooked the door and they went in. They had been walking towards the sun on the way down. The barn was black as night in contrast and warm from the hay and from the beasts. Jody's father moved over towards the one box stall. 'Come here!' he ordered. Jody could begin to see things now. He looked into the box stall and then stepped back quickly.   5

A red pony colt was looking at him out of the stall. Its tense ears were forward and a light of disobedience was in its eyes. Its coat was rough and thick as an Airedale's fur and its mane was long and tangled. Jody's throat collapsed in on itself and cut his breath short.   10

'He needs a good currying,' his father said, 'and if I ever hear of you not feeding him or leaving his stall dirty, I'll sell him off in a minute.'

Jody couldn't bear to look at the pony's eyes any more. He gazed down at his hands for a moment, and he asked very shyly: 'Mine?' No one answered him. He put his hand out towards the pony. Its grey nose   15
came close, sniffing loudly, and then the lips drew back and the strong teeth closed on Jody's fingers. The pony shook its head up and down and seemed to laugh with amusement. Jody regarded his bruised fingers. 'Well,' he said with pride – 'well, I guess he can bite all right.' The two men laughed, somewhat in relief. Carl Tiflin went out of the   20
barn and walked up a side-hill to be by himself, for he was embarrassed, but Billy Buck stayed. It was easier to talk to Billy Buck. Jody asked again – 'Mine?'

Billy became professional in tone. 'Sure! That is, if you look out for him and break him right. I'll show you how. He's just a colt. You can't   25
ride him for some time.'

Jody put out his bruised hand again, and this time the red pony let his nose be rubbed.

1. Jody went to the stable with both his father and Billy.
   (TRUE/FALSE)

2. Their visit to the barn took place at night.
   (TRUE/FALSE)

3. The only animal in the barn was the red pony.
   (TRUE/FALSE)

4. Jody 'stepped back quickly' (line 5) because he was startled by the pony.
   (TRUE/FALSE)

5. The red pony was doing all the following: looking at Jody; listening intensely; waiting to bite Jody.
   (TRUE/FALSE)

6. The pony's coat was compared with that of a dog.
   (TRUE/FALSE)

7. Jody's 'throat collapsed in on itself' (line 10) because of fear.
   (TRUE/FALSE)

8. The word 'currying', as used in line 11, means 'rubbing down and dressing'.
   (TRUE/FALSE)

9. The implication of the remark, 'and if I ever hear of you not feeding him or leaving his stall dirty' (lines 11–12) is that Jody's father was giving him the pony.
   (TRUE/FALSE)

10. Jody could not bear to look at the pony's eyes any more, (line 13) because they 'contained a light of disobedience'.

(TRUE/FALSE)

11. Jody 'gazed down at his hands for a moment' (lines 13–14) because he was overcome by his emotions.

(TRUE/FALSE)

12. The pony bit Jody's fingers out of spite.

(TRUE/FALSE)

13. Jody spoke 'with pride' (line 19) because he was pleased to own such a spirited pony.

(TRUE/FALSE)

14. The two men 'laughed, somewhat in relief' (line 20) because they had been uncertain how Jody would react to the pony.

(TRUE/FALSE)

15. Carl Tiflin 'was embarrassed' (line 22) because the pony had bitten Jody on their first meeting.

(TRUE/FALSE)

16. Billy Buck was obviously Carl Tiflin's employee who looked after the horses.

(TRUE/FALSE)

17. The word 'break' (line 25) refers to the way horses are tamed and made obedient.

(TRUE/FALSE)

18. Billy said that Jody could not ride the colt for some time because the horse was too young.

(TRUE/FALSE)

19. The pony 'let his nose be rubbed' (lines 27–28) because it realised Jody was now his new owner.

(TRUE/FALSE)

20. The name of the boy in the passage was Jody Buck.

(TRUE/FALSE)

Exercise 13

The Start of a Trial

The King and Queen of Hearts were seated on their throne with a great crowd assembled about them – all sorts of little birds and beasts, as well as the whole pack of cards: the Knave was standing before them, in chains, with a soldier on each side to guard him; and near the King was

the White Rabbit, with a trumpet in one hand and a scroll of 5
parchment in the other. In the very middle of the court was a table,
with a large dish of tarts upon it: they looked so good, that it made Alice
quite hungry to look at them.

'I wish they'd get the trial done,' she thought, 'and hand round the
refreshments!' But there seemed no chance of this; so she began 10
looking at everything about her to pass away the time.

Alice had never been in a court of justice before, but she had read
about them in books, and she was quite pleased to find that she knew
the name of everything there. 'That's the judge,' she said to herself,
'because of his great wig.' As he wore his crown over the wig, he did not 15
look at all comfortable and it was certainly not becoming.

'And that's the jury-box,' thought Alice; 'and those twelve
creatures,' (she was obliged to say 'creatures', you see, because some of
them were animals and some were birds,) 'I suppose they are the
jurors.' 20

The twelve jurors were all writing very busily on their slates.

'What are they doing?' Alice whispered to the Gryphon. 'They can't
have anything put down yet, before the trial's begun.'

'They're putting down their names,' the Gryphon whispered in
reply, 'for fear they should forget them before the end of the trial.' 25

'Stupid things!' Alice began in a loud indignant voice; but she
stopped herself hastily, for the White Rabbit cried out, 'Silence in the
court!' and the King put on his spectacles and looked anxiously round
to make out who was talking.

Alice could see, as well as if she were looking over their shoulders, 30
that all the jurors were writing down 'Stupid things!' on their slates,
and she could even make out that one of them didn't know how to spell
'stupid'.

One of the jurors had a pencil that squeaked. This, of course, Alice
could *not* stand, and she went round the court and got behind him, and 35
very soon found an opportunity of taking it away.

'Herald, read the accusation!' said the King.

On this the herald blew three blasts on the trumpet and then
unrolled the parchment-scroll and read as follows:

> *'The Queen of Hearts, she made some tarts,* 40
>   *All on a summer day:*
> *The Knave of Hearts, he stole those tarts*
>   *And took them quite away!'*

'Consider your verdict,' the King said to the jury.

'Not yet, not yet!' the Rabbit hastily interrupted. 'There's a great 45
deal to come before that!'

'Wake up, Alice dear!' said her sister. 'Why, what a sleep you had.'

1. The story of the trial is really a dream.
   (TRUE/FALSE)

2. The jury consisted of birds, beasts, and a whole pack of cards.
   (TRUE/FALSE)

3. There were two soldiers guarding the accused.
   (TRUE/FALSE)

4. The accused were the Knave of Hearts and the White Rabbit.
   (TRUE/FALSE)

5. The large dish of tarts was on the table for the Court's refreshments.
   (TRUE/FALSE)

6. Alice realised the tarts really were the evidence for the robbery.
   (TRUE/FALSE)

7. Alice knew everything about courts of justice because she read a lot.
   (TRUE/FALSE)

8. The judge was the king.
   (TRUE/FALSE)

9. The king seemed ill at ease and not very attractive.
   (TRUE/FALSE)

10. Alice called the twelve jurors 'creatures' (line 18) because she disapproved of them.
    (TRUE/FALSE)

11. Alice was surprised the jurors were busy writing because they were animals and birds.
    (TRUE/FALSE)

12. Alice called the jurors 'Stupid things!' (line 26) because they started writing before the trial began.
    (TRUE/FALSE)

13. When Alice called the jurors 'Stupid things!' (line 26) she spoke in a way that showed she was scornful and angry.
    (TRUE/FALSE)

14. Alice knew what the jurors were writing down because she was looking over their shoulders.
    (TRUE/FALSE)

15. The juror who 'had a pencil that squeaked' (line 34) was the one who could not spell.
    (TRUE/FALSE)

16. The word *not* is printed in italics (line 35) to emphasise that before she got up Alice had been sitting down.

(TRUE/FALSE)

17. Alice went behind the juror with the squeaky pencil (line 35) so that she could make a surprise attack on him.

(TRUE/FALSE)

18. The Herald who read the accusation in court was the White Rabbit.

(TRUE/FALSE)

19. After the accusation had been read, the King asked the jury to consider the evidence.

(TRUE/FALSE)

20. The Rabbit hastily interrupted the King (line 45) because the trial had not begun.

(TRUE/FALSE)

Exercise 14

The Birth of Reggae

Reggae was born in the night-time slum streets of Kingston, Jamaica, the pure black music of the black poor. Whereas the Blues, although forged in a similar poverty, was almost always the individual voice of individual misfortune, reggae, at its roots is the sound and the language of broader and more urgent social awareness and aspirations.   5

The lyrics at the roots of reggae are edgy and unsentimental, firmly based in the realities of hunger, poverty, passion, prison, oppression, retribution and vengeance; many are about Ethiopia, symbolic home of free black people, and about Selassie, hereditary king of free black people, the symbolic representative of black men as they were meant to   10
be; free and dignified, the rightful heirs to all that is theirs, people with the power and the history to determine the directions of their own futures. The rhythm is compulsive, sometimes even monotonously regular, which, by contrast, points up rather than dulls down the bitterness of the lyrics.   15

The evolution of the sound of reggae is part and parcel of the blackness of its creators. Although born in Kingston, reggae's ancestors were in Africa long before it was incubated by the heavy rhythms of rural Jamaican revivalist meetings. It was developed, however, by musicians who, shoeless for the large part, were growing   20
increasingly aware of blackness, by men who made their own saxophones and violins from bamboo tubes, their guitars from empty cigar boxes (with elastic bands or thin, salvaged wire for strings) and complex rhythm sections from discarded crates and deep-chested tea cases.   25

1. Reggae, as a musical form, came into existence in the night clubs of Kingston, Jamaica.
   (TRUE/FALSE)

2. Both reggae and the blues had their origins among deprived, black communities.
   (TRUE/FALSE)

3. The main difference between reggae and the blues as they began was that the blues impressed the sadness of an individual man or woman and reggae expressed hopes for a better society in general.
   (TRUE/FALSE)

4. The word 'lyrics' (line 6) refers to the heavy beat of reggae.
   (TRUE/FALSE)

5. The lyrics of reggae express the facts about suffering and the bitter reaction to it sharply and without deliberately exaggerating emotions.
   (TRUE/FALSE)

6. The lyrics of reggae express all the following, among other things: deprivation, famine, violent emotions, enslavement, and revenge.
   (TRUE/FALSE)

7. Ethiopia was the country from which all black people in Jamaica came originally.
   (TRUE/FALSE)

8. Selassie was once king of Ethiopia and the symbol of the liberty and dignity of black races.
   (TRUE/FALSE)

9. The word 'hereditary' (line 9) means 'acknowledged'.
   (TRUE/FALSE)

10. Selassie seemed to symbolise the independence, the dignity, and the right to self-determination of black people.
    (TRUE/FALSE)

11. The word 'compulsive' as used in line 13 means 'irresistibly compelling'.
    (TRUE/FALSE)

12. According to the passage, the monotonously regular rhythm of reggae accentuates the sharpness of some of the lyrics.
    (TRUE/FALSE)

13. In the second paragraph the writer argues that reggae can bring about social and political revolutions.
    (TRUE/FALSE)

14. The words 'part and parcel of' (line 16) serve to emphasise that the way reggae developed was intricately bound up with the fact that its creators were black.

(TRUE/FALSE)

15. The passage suggests that the very beginnings of reggae are to be found in revivalist meetings in Jamaica.

(TRUE/FALSE)

16. According to lines 19–25, reggae was developed by poor musicians who had not realised before that they were black.

(TRUE/FALSE)

17. The musicians who developed reggae in Jamaica made improvised instruments mainly from materials that had been thrown away because they were poor.

(TRUE/FALSE)

18. The early reggae bands included wind, stringed and percussion instruments.

(TRUE/FALSE)

19. The main musical quality of reggae stressed in the passage is the contrast between its heavy, monotonously regular rhythms and the sharpness of its words expressing suffering, determination and hopes.

(TRUE/FALSE)

20. The passage is mainly concerned with comparing the development of reggae with the development of the blues.

(TRUE/FALSE)

Exercise 15

A Firework Display

By the car stand two women with a police-dog on a chain, The dog, alert, nervous, uneasy, crouches and then rises restlessly. *Bang*! Up goes the first rocket, like a golden tadpole wiggling up in the sky; then a burst of red and green sparks. The dog winces, and crouches under the running-board of the car. *Bang*! *Bang*! *Crackle*! More rockets, more   5
showers of stars and fizzes of light in the sky. The dog whimpers; his mistresses divide their attention between the heavens and him. In the sky, the moon draws further and further off, while still watching palely. Nearer in the high sky, a rolling and fuming of smoke, a whistling of rockets, a spangling and splashing of coloured lights, and, most   10
impressively of all, the continuous explosions within the air itself, the high air bursting outwards from within itself, in continual shocks. It is more like an air-raid than anything.

The dog suffers and suffers more. He tries to hide away, not to look
at all. But there is an extra bang and a fusillade! He has to look! He   15
shivers like a glass cup that is going to shatter. His mistresses try to
comfort him. They want to look at the fireworks but their interest in
the dog is more real. And he, he wants to cover his ears, and bury his
head, but at every new bang he starts afresh and rises, turns round.
Sometimes he sits like a statue of pure distress, still as bronze. Then he   20
curls away upon himself again, curling to get away, while the high sky
bursts and reverberates, wiggles with tadpoles of golden fire, and
plunges with splashes of light, spangles of colour.

1. It is clear that the police-dog is 'uneasy' (line 2) because he is on a
   chain.

   (TRUE/FALSE)

2. The dog described in lines 1–2 seems to be all the following: anxious,
   wide-awake, and agitated.

   (TRUE/FALSE)

3. The word '*Bang*' in line 2 describes the sound made by the rocket as
   it explodes in the sky.

   (TRUE/FALSE)

4. The first rocket (line 3) is compared with a tadpole because of its
   colour and the way it moves in the sky.

   (TRUE/FALSE)

5. The word 'winces' (line 4) describes the way the police-dog runs for
   cover.

   (TRUE/FALSE)

6. The dog 'crouches under the running-board of the car' (lines 4–5)
   mainly to avoid the sparks falling from the rocket.

   (TRUE/FALSE)

7. The word 'fizzes' (line 6) mainly describes the noise made by the
   bursting of the rockets.

   (TRUE/FALSE)

8. 'Whimpers' (line 6) is used by the writer to suggest that the dog is
   making a frightened, mournful sound.

   (TRUE/FALSE)

9. The dog's mistresses ignore their animal because they are watching
   the firework display.

   (TRUE/FALSE)

10. 'The moon draws further and further off' (line 8) because its light
    seems weak as the fireworks explode.

    (TRUE/FALSE)

11. The writer finds the dazzling colours the most impressive thing about the firework display.
    (TRUE/FALSE)

12. The firework display 'is more like an air-raid than anything' (lines 12–13) because of the way the rockets explode continuously.
    (TRUE/FALSE)

13. The word 'tries' (line 14) suggests that the dog does not succeed in hiding away completely.
    (TRUE/FALSE)

14. The comparison of the way the rockets explode with a 'fusillade' (line 15) shows that they make one huge bang.
    (TRUE/FALSE)

15. The dog 'has to look' (line 15) because he is surprised by an explosion he does not expect.
    (TRUE/FALSE)

16. The comparison of the way the dog shivers and 'a glass cup that is going to shatter' (line 16) refers to the way a high-pitched noise can break a glass once it reaches a particular frequency.
    (TRUE/FALSE)

17. As the firework display continues, the dog's mistresses care more for their animal than watching the rockets.
    (TRUE/FALSE)

18. The way the dog reacts to the continued firework display suggests he is a very timid animal.
    (TRUE/FALSE)

19. The word 'bronze' (line 20) is used deliberately to emphasise the contrast between the way the dog curls down with the way the sky bursts and reverberates above.
    (TRUE/FALSE)

20. The description of the firework display and the dog's reaction is given from the point of view of the mistresses of the animal.
    (TRUE/FALSE)

Chapter 3

DIY or Do-it-Yourself item-writing

1. The secret of success in finding the answers to questions in Comprehension exercises lies in reading *both* the passage *and* the questions very carefully indeed before trying to decide on your answers.

   In some tests the questions take the form of **multiple-choice items**. These give a number of possible answers which might occur to an intelligent person who has read the passage very closely, but only one of the possible answers (or **options**, as they are called) is correct or the best.

What kinds of objective tests?

2. It will be helpful if we begin by explaining a few technical terms used in objective tests before trying to construct a few questions for ourselves.

   (*a*) An **item** is a question to see whether you have understood one specific point about what you have read.

   (*b*) The first part of an item is **the stem**. This consists of one of the following:

       (*i*) *a direct question*: *e.g.* 'Which one of the following is closest in meaning to 'pneumonoultramicroscopicsilicovolcanoconiosis'* as used in line 1?'

       (*The longest word in English!)

       (*ii*) *a statement* which has to be completed: *e.g.* 'Floccinaucinihilipilification', as used in line 2, is an action which. . . .

       (*iii*) *a direction*: *e.g.* Say which *one* of the following best explains what is meant by 'antidisestablishmentarianism', as used in line 3.

   (*c*) The options (sometimes called **the responses**) are suggested answers to the question. Usually there are four or five options in an item, but there may be as few as three or as many as six.

   (*d*) **The key** is the correct or the best option of those given. The other options are called **distractors** – since they try to distract you from the key.

Finding the keys and spotting the distractors

3. How can you be sure of choosing the right key?

   (*a*) It is essential to read the passage and the item very closely indeed.

The key will emerge as the *only possible* correct or best choice for you to make from the options, if you apply to the question your own knowledge of the English language and think hard about what words mean in a very particular and specific context.

(*b*) Read the options carefully; if you have read the passage correctly the key should be obvious straightaway. You may have to re-read the appropriate part of the passage again – even several times. If you still cannot find the key you will have to begin a process of elimination: *i.e.* deciding which options are definitely 'distractors'. This process should allow you to reduce the 'possible' keys on which to concentrate.

If you run into serious difficulties in tests or examinations, it is usually best to go on to the next item. Not only will this help you to finish the test in time but it will also allow your mind to continue working quietly over the difficulty. Often, when you turn back to the problem item, you will find you can spot the key without any further trouble.

What are the questions (or items) likely to ask?

4. Objective tests in English Language normally try to find out how skilful you are in the following areas:

   (*a*) **Inference**: drawing conclusions about what is actually written.

   (*b*) **Vocabulary**: understanding how words are used with special meanings *in special contexts.*

   (*c*) **Summary**: summing up the main points in a description or a discussion.

   (*d*) **Comprehension**: establishing what a passage *actually says and means.* Bear in mind that sometimes the words cannot be taken at their face value but have deeper, richer, or more involved meanings than may exist on the surface. (*e.g.* 'You're a pig!' doesn't mean that you really are an animal with four cloven feet, a snout, two strange ears, and a curly tail!)

   (*e*) **Idiom**: understanding the way words and phrases are used in English by those whose mother tongue is English. (*e.g.* the German equivalent of 'He's got bats in the belfry' is 'He has caterpillars in the head'; the French sometimes say, 'He has a spider up on the ceiling'!)

   (*f*) **Figurative language**: appreciating the width and richness of interpretation in expressions using figures of speech – especially those involving comparisons of one thing with another.

   (*g*) **Deduction** or **reasoning**: working out the steps in an argument and spotting any false statements.

   (*h*) **Punctuation**: recognising the way punctuation marks (*e.g. inverted commas*) or *underlining* (or *italicising*) can affect meaning.

These are also the areas that the more old-fashioned, open-ended questions tried to cover in Comprehension tests. In examinations, of course, items which have already been thoroughly pre-tested and which are reliable, can be marked with 100 per cent accuracy by a computer, so that those taking the tests can be certain that their work will be assessed without any risk of mistakes being made by examiners.

What kinds of item are there?

5. In English, of course, often there is not one single answer to a question – especially if it is asking about inferences or figurative language. To allow for this, four main kinds of item are used in English Comprehension tests, in addition to those which ask for a simple *True/False* response. (**See Chapter Two.**) In the following descriptions the examples are given merely to illustrate *the form* items might take. Remember that in a test the only way to find the key to an item is to refer it back to the passage on which it is based.

(a) The simple question item

Here the *stem* asks a clear, straightforward, direct question. The options provide possible answers for you to consider but only one, the key, is the correct or best answer.

e.g. Why did the chicken cross the road?
* A To get to the other side
  B To buy some bright new feathers
  C To escape from the mad butcher
  D To talk to a turkey there
  E To confuse the traffic passing by
  (* The key.)

(b) The simple completion item

Here the *stem* takes the form of an unfinished statement and the options provide possible ways of completing it. The key will provide the best way to do this.

e.g. The chicken crossed the road because it wanted to
  A buy some bright new feathers
  B escape from the mad butcher
  C talk to a turkey there
  D confuse the traffic passing by
* E get to the other side
  (* The key.)

(c) The multiple completion item

Here the *stem* may take the form of either a question or an unfinished statement but two or even three of the suggested answers taken together will provide the key.

e.g. (*a*) Which *two* of the following are animals?
  1. A muid
  2. An izard
  3. A poon
  4. An adobe
  5. A kudu

  A 1 and 2 only
  B 1 and 4 only
  C 2 and 5 only
  D 3 and 4 only
  E 3 and 5 only
(You will probably need a dictionary to find the key here!)

e.g. (*b*) Which *three* of the following are the names of plants?
  1. Pigsconce
  2. Lords and Ladies
  3. Lesser Dodder
  4. Cats and dogs
  5. Horehound

  A 1, 2, and 4 only
  B 1, 2, and 5 only
  C 1, 3, and 4 only
  D 2, 3, and 5 only
  E 3, 4, and 5 only
(You will need the dictionary again! Remember, however, that in a test you would have to refer the question back to the passage. The dictionary will help you sometimes but it is not an infallible way of determining what a word means *in a particular context*.)

(*d*) The EXCEPT item.

This is similar to the multiple-completion kinds of item but here ALL the options are correct EXCEPT one. You are looking for the odd one out, therefore, as the key.

e.g. All the following are names of place names in England EXCEPT
  A Kneesup
  B Baldon Toot and Marsh
  C Shellow Bowells
  D Lower and Upper Swell
  E Inkpen

(Look up these names in the book such as the *Concise Oxford Dictionary of English Place-Names* found in most libraries.)

Exercise 16

In the items in this exercise the keys are missing but the distractors are given. Using dictionaries and other reference books find keys for yourself which you can justify. (Make sure that your *key* is the same shape as the other options or your answer will draw attention to itself because it is too long, too short, has too many words, or simply looks different.)

1. In which year was the first General Assembly of the United Nations Organisation held?
   A 1919
   B 1925
   C 1938
   D —
   E 1952

2. Which one of the following is a term *not* used in Computer Studies?
   A Keystrokes
   B Floppy disc
   C Ram capacity
   D —
   E Daisywheels
   Can you rewrite the stem of this item to turn it into a multiple-completion **EXCEPT** item?

3. The term *knock-on* is one used in the sport of
   A lacrosse
   B basket-ball
   C hockey
   D base-ball
   E —

4. The words *to curry* are ones you are most likely to use in the hobby of
   A hill-climbing
   B —
   C dressmaking
   D stamp-collecting
   E train-spotting

5. All the following are examples of idiomatic phrases in English **EXCEPT**:
   A It was raining cats and dogs.
   B I have a bone in my leg.
   C He played his cards very well.
   D She bought a real pig in a poke.
   E ——

6. Which *three* of the following are well-known sayings in English?
   1. After the rain comes the good weather.
   2. It never rains but it pours.
   3. ———
   4. Birds of a feather flock together.
   5. It's the drop which makes the barrel overflow.

   A 1, 2, and 3 only
   B 1, 2, and 5 only
   C 2, 3, and 4 only
   D 2, 4, and 5 only
   E 3, 4, and 5 only

   (C will be the key)

   (NB. 1. is a literal translation of a French saying: *après la pluie le beau temps* and 5 a literal translation of a German saying: *es ist der Tropfen, der das Fasz zum Überlaufen bringt*. What are the English equivalents of these sayings?)

7. All the following groups of letters refer to well-known international organisations EXCEPT
   A ———
   B WHO
   C UNO
   D WMO
   E ILO

   (Find another three-letter group for your key which ends in — O and is in fact a real abbreviation, although it is *not* one which refers to an international organisation (*e.g.* UFO); a section at the end of a good dictionary normally lists abbreviations.) Can you rewrite this item in the form of a *simple question* item?

8. Which *one* of the following words best fills the gap in the following explanation of the idiomatic English phrase *To run the gauntlet*?

   The reference is to a punishment in the armed forces; the soldiers or sailors, provided with rope ends, were drawn up in two rows facing each other and the — had to run between them while every man hit him as hard as he could.

   A Accused
   B Suspect
   C ———
   D Defendant
   E Traitor

9. Which *one* of the following words is the most likely to have been omitted from the following news item?

Police arrested about 41 protestors on bicycles, who were among 150 people — against cruise missiles by repeatedly cycling round Grosvenor Square, Mayfair, where the US Embassy is sited, and Parliament Square.

A Fighting
B Shouting
C Rebelling
D Marching
E ——

10. All the following are traditionally thought to be the very last words spoken by famous people EXCEPT
A 'I feel the flowers growing over me.' (John Keats)
B 'I shall hear in heaven.' (Beethoven, who was deaf)
C —————— (Alfred the Great*)
D 'While there is life there is hope.' (The father of the Brontë sisters)
E 'Die, my dear doctor! That's the *last* thing I shall do.' (Palmerston)

(* If you wish, you can alter the name here to that of another famous person. If you try to be too funny, you will draw too much attention to your key! The distractors can be verified by checking them in a book such as *Brewer's Dictionary of Phrase and Fable*.

Exercise 17

In the items in this exercise some or all of the distractors are missing but the keys are given. Using what you have learnt in this chapter about the ways items can be constructed find suitable distractors of your own. (Make sure that the distractors you find do not draw attention to themselves because of their shape; remember that they must appear, at least at first glance, to be possibly correct but they must not conflict with the key.)

1. Which one of the following is closest in meaning to *pneumonoultramicroscopicsilicovolcanoconiosis?*
A ——
B ——
C A serious lung disease caused by inhaling very fine quartz dust.
D ——
E ——

2. Which *one* of the following is closest in meaning to 'A rolling stone gathers no moss'?
A ——
B ——
C ——
D ——
E One who never settles down will never be rich.

3. 'A good Samaritan' is a person who
   A comes to the aid of others in need, whatever the cost
   B ——
   C ——
   D ——
   E ——

4. Which one of the following words best fills the gap in the idiomatic expression 'He was sailing very close to the —'?
   A ——
   B ——
   C ——
   D Wind
   E ——

5. Which *two* of the following games make use of a ball?
   1 Ice-hockey
   2 Fives
   3 ——
   4 Mahjongg
   5 Pelota

   A 1 and 2 only
   B 1 and 4 only
   C 2 and 5 only
   D 3 and 4 only
   E 3 and 5 only

   (**C** will be the key.)

6. Which three of the following abbreviations refer to honours and awards given for distinguished services?
   1 CBE
   2 CVO
   3 CID
   4 ——
   5 CMG

   A 1, 2, and 3 only
   B 1, 2, and 5 only
   C 1, 3, and 4 only
   D 2, 4, and 5 only
   E 3, 4, and 5 only

   (**B** will be the key.)

(A section at the end of a good dictionary normally lists abbreviations.)

7. Which *three* of the following are English idioms?
    1 She helped a lame dog over a stile.
    2 I have other cats to whip.†
    3 The thief was in for a penny in for a pound.
    4 ——
    5 He entered the kitchen like a bull in a china shop.

    A 1, 2, and 3 only
    B 1, 2, and 4 only
    C 1, 3, and 5 only
    D 2, 4, and 5 only
    E 3, 4, and 5 only

                                        (C will be the key.)
    (†This is a literal translation of the French: *j'ai d'autres chats à fouetter*;
    the English equivalent is, 'I have other fish to fry'.)

8. Read the following news item and then say which word is the most likely
   to have been omitted from it.

    A Mogadishu court sentenced four Somalis to be executed by firing
    squad for stealing 17m shillings (£740,000) from public funds.
    They were also — by the court to pay it back.

    A asked
    B ordered
    C ——
    D obliged
    E forced

                                        (B is the key,)

9. All the following are words meaning 'a male person' which are more
   likely to be used in informal English (or in slang) than in formal writing
   EXCEPT
    A bloke
    B chap
    C guy
    D ——
    E man

                                        (E is the key.)

10. All the following are more likely to be written in prose rather than in
    verse EXCEPT
    A a novel
    B ——
    C a report
    D a diary
    E a ballad

                                        (E is the key.)

Part Two

Objective tests and development work

Exploration 1

Map-reading

I. Study the following map carefully and then answer the questions which follow. *DO NOT GUESS.*

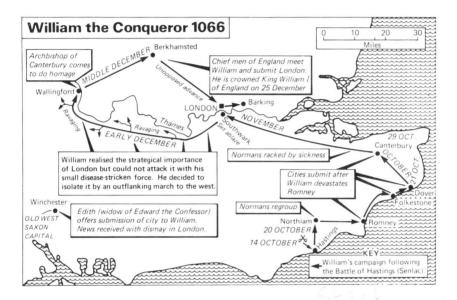

William the Conqueror 1066

Archbishop of Canterbury comes to do homage

Berkhamsted

MIDDLE DECEMBER

Unopposed advance

Chief men of England meet William and submit London. He is crowned King William I of England on 25 December

Wallingford

LONDON

Barking

Ravaging

Thames

Ravaging

EARLY DECEMBER

Southwark Set ablaze

NOVEMBER

29 OCT.
Canterbury

OCTOBER

21 OCT.

Normans racked by sickness

William realised the strategical importance of London but could not attack it with his small disease-stricken force. He decided to isolate it by an outflanking march to the west.

Cities submit after William devastates Romney

Dover
Folkestone

Winchester

OLD WEST SAXON CAPITAL

Edith (widow of Edward the Confessor) offers submission of city to William. News received with dismay in London.

Normans regroup

Romney

Northiam
20 OCTOBER

14 OCTOBER

Hastings

KEY

William's campaign following the Battle of Hastings (Senlac).

0   10   20   30
Miles

1. How long did it take for William the Conqueror to be crowned King of England from the date of the Battle of Hastings?
   A 30 days
   B 46 days
   C 57 days
   D 73 days
   E 81 days

2. Which one of the following stopped William the Conqueror from making a direct attack on London?
   A Collaboration
   B Resistance
   C Defeat
   D Illness
   E Surrender

3. Which two of the following acknowledged defeat by William the Conqueror's army before the final surrender?

1. A Queen of England
2. Members of Parliament
3. The Archbishop of Canterbury
4. Citizens of London
5. The Chief Men of England

A 1 and 2 only
B 1 and 3 only
C 2 and 5 only
D 3 and 4 only
E 4 and 5 only

4. William the Conqueror wished to capture London as soon as possible because it
   A was the capital of England
   B lay directly in his path
   C threatened his army's eastern flank
   D would give him a decisive advantage
   E was full of riches to plunder

5. William the Conqueror ravaged along the Thames and attacked Wallingford because
   A he wanted to weaken English resistance bit by bit
   B the centre of government was to be found in Winchester
   C he wanted to conquer the South-East of England by fear
   D the Norman soldiers demanded an opportunity to ravage and pillage
   E he wanted to avoid a direct assault on London.

The Highway Code

II. Read the following passage taken from *The Highway Code* carefully and then answer the questions which follow. *DO NOT GUESS.*

To Pedal Cyclists

Before cycling, *make sure that*
– your cycle has efficient brakes
You *must*, even if you are wheeling your cycle,
– observe amber and red 'Stop' signals, traffic signs which give orders, double white lines, yellow road markings and the directions of a police constable (or traffic warden) controlling traffic;
– stop when signalled to do so by a School Crossing Patrol exhibiting a 'Stop-Children' sign;
– give precedence to pedestrians on a push-button controlled crossing, when an amber light is flashing.

You *must*

– at night, see that your front and rear lamps are alight and that your cycle has an efficient red rear reflector;
– at night, if you are wheeling your cycle or are stationary without lights, keep as close as possible to the nearside edge of the road;
– stop when required to do so by a police constable (or traffic warden) in uniform.

You *must not*

– stop your cycle within the limits of a pedestrian crossing, except in circumstances beyond your control or when it is necessary to do so to avoid an accident;
– on the approach to an uncontrolled Zebra crossing marked by a pattern of zigzag lines, overtake the moving motor vehicle nearest to the crossing or the leading vehicle which has stopped to give way to a pedestrian on the crossing;
– ride recklessly;
– ride without due care and attention or without reasonable consideration for other persons using the road;
– ride under the influence of drink or a drug;
– wilfully ride on a footpath by the side of any road made or set apart for the use of foot passengers;
– by negligence or misbehaviour interrupt the free passage of any road user or vehicle;
– leave your cycle on any road in such a way that is likely to cause danger to other road users;
– leave your cycle where waiting is prohibited;
– carry a passenger on a bicycle not constructed or adapted to carry more than one person;
– hold on to a motor vehicle or trailer in motion on any road.

6. According to the Highway Code, your cycle must be in a condition to allow you to
   A ride comfortably
   B stop effectively
   C park safely
   D swerve suddenly
   E ride fast

7. As a cyclist you are required by law to do all the following *EXCEPT*
   A ride with due care and attention
   B obey official traffic signals and road markings
   C give pedestrians priority at all times
   D observe lighting regulations after lighting-up time
   E keep off footpaths by the roadside

8. You are required as a cyclist by law to stop for all the following *EXCEPT*
   - **(A)** police in plain clothes
   - **B** traffic signals
   - **C** school crossing patrols
   - **D** traffic wardens
   - **E** pedestrians on crossings

9. When you are riding a cycle you must by law be all the following *EXCEPT*
   - **A** careful
   - **B** sober
   - **(C)** polite
   - **D** responsible
   - **E** considerate

10. Which *one* of the following cyclists would necessarily be breaking the law? One who
    - **A** rides along carrying a passenger
    - **(B)** ignores amber lights on crossings
    - **C** carries no lighting equipment
    - **D** impedes cars anxious to overtake
    - **E** rides on paths at the roadside

Development

Further reading

1. *The Highway Code*, HMSO
2. R. Church, *Over the Bridge*, New Windmill Series, Heinemann Educational Books, 1966.
   (*Chapter Fifteen* gives an amusing account of a cycle ride and an unfortunate accident.)

Activities

1. Draw a map of the immediate area in which you live; show the road system, the main features (*e.g.* churches, public houses, commons, memorials, schools, etc.
2. Describe, with the help of an illustrative map, your route to school or college every day.
3. Draw a historical map to describe a battle or exploration given in your history textbook.

Written work

1. Give an account *either* of a cycle trip you once undertook *or* of an incident you had as a pedestrian involving a cyclist.
2. Invent a set of instructions for pedestrians and car-drivers which you, as a cyclist, would like to see implemented as law. (Use the style of *The Highway Code*, if you wish.)

Exploration 2

The following is an advertisement from a Sunday colour supplement for a home computer system. Read it very carefully, bearing in mind that it is an advertisement trying to sell a product. Then answer the questions which follow. *DO NOT GUESS.*

A Home Computer

1. If you know about personal computers, you know about the great reputation of the Apple IIe.

But what you may not know is that now we've made the IIe attainable as an element of our unique Professional Home Computer Package.

So you won't need the bank manager's blessing before buying one.

2. THE PROFESSIONAL HOME COMPUTER YOU'LL NEVER GROW OUT OF.

With around $1\frac{1}{4}$ million machines in use worldwide, the Apple II is the most popular of all professional computers, and it's easy to see why.

Features include a full-size keyboard, and a king-size 64k memory, which can itself be doubled with an auxiliary card.

A range of printers is also readily available, just part of the comprehensive and compatible family of Apple-branded hardware.

Making your Apple IIe highly versatile and hugely expandable, to develop with your needs.

You can use it directly in conjunction with your television set, or if you require extra clarity for high-resolution text, with the special Apple II monitor.

3. ALL THE ADVANTAGES OF DISK DRIVE.

Disk drive means speed and reliability. It enables you to access any of your programs of data-files almost at once, without having to run through them all to find what you want.

Not to mention the fact that the best programs are written for disk.

Which is why Apple disk-based systems are the standard for business. And why disk drive lifts you far above the limitations of cassettes and micro-drives.

4. THE CHOICE OF SOFTWARE YOU'LL NEVER EXHAUST.

The impressive technical specifications of the Apple IIe are matched by its range of software.

The widest, most extensive range available, in fact, numbering over 20,000 separate packages.

Naturally, there are plenty of games and educational programs.

But the particular strength of the Apple IIe lies in its more sophisticated software applications.

While the Professional Home Computer Package gives unique value with privileged purchase arrangements on important items.

Such as Apple Logo, the programming language for all ages and abilities.

Such as Applewriter, which turns your machine into a sophisticated word processor.

And such as QuickFile, designed to help you manage important everyday information.

5. ALL THE BENEFITS OF PRESTEL.

You no longer need to buy a special set to access Prestel.

The Professional Home Computer Package includes a voucher towards all the equipment you require to link into Prestel at a huge saving.

Opening up wide vistas of information and interest for you to browse.

Including access to Micronet 800, your own closed user group within Prestel. You ca even download software from Micronet into your Apple computer.

6. THE TRAINING AIDS YOU'LL NEVER IMPROVE UPON.

You'll want to get the most you can from your IIe.

The package contains the 'Apple presents Apple' disk, teaching you all the keyboard basics, as well as a superb instruction manual which deals with the system in greater depth.

If you wish to learn BASIC, a manual is available for that purpose too.

There is also the option of a free professional computer training course, so you'll be able to use your machine better, sooner.

There are a variety of courses to choose from, all held in Authorised Apple Training Centres throughout the country.

The Apple Professional Home Computer Package. At around £998 or less, how can you afford to buy anything else?

I. The following twelve questions require a True/False answer.

1. *The first section* flatters the reader by suggesting that he is probably knowledgeable about home computers.

(TRUE/FALSE)

2. *The first section's* conclusion ('So you won't need the bank manager's blessing before you buy one') follows logically and inevitably from the previous paragraph.

(TRUE/FALSE)

3. *The second section* opens with a claim about the popularity of the whole computer package which the advertisement is designed to sell.

(TRUE/FALSE)

4. *The second section* can be understood easily even by those without any knowledge at all of computers.

(TRUE/FALSE)

5. *The third section* increases very markedly the use of technical language.

(TRUE/FALSE)

6. *The third section* emphasises the use of the computer system in business as well as the home.

(TRUE/FALSE)

7. *The fourth section* emphasises the versatility and the usefulness to everyone of the computer package advertised.

(TRUE/FALSE)

8. *The fourth section* also suggests that the computer is cheap to purchase.

(TRUE/FALSE)

9. *The fifth section* indicates that the computer package will allow you free access to the Prestel information bank.

(TRUE/FALSE)

10. *The sixth section* points out that a manual teaching you the fundamental operating skills comes with the equipment.

(TRUE/FALSE)

11. *The sixth section* indicates that the computer package is backed up by training courses for those who wish to use the equipment for professional purposes.

(TRUE/FALSE)

12. *The sixth section* ends with a question to which the advertiser hopes the reader will give an answer such as, 'Of course not!'

(TRUE/FALSE)

II. The following twenty questions are objective-test items with only one of the 'options' to each question correct. Find this key **without guessing** but by reading the text closely.

Questions based on the first section

1. The first paragraph stresses that the personal computer advertised is
   A reliable
   B useful
   C famous
   D cheap

2. Which one of the following words is closest in meaning to 'unique' as used in this section?
   A Formidable
   B Incomparable
   C Attainable
   D Indescribable

3. The last sentence ('So you won't need . . . before buying one') is intended to suggest to you, as the reader, that

A bank managers would advise against such purchases
B the whole package is within your financial resources
C the advantages would quickly offset the cost
D bank managers would provide you with the finance

Questions based on the second section

4. The first paragraph suggests mainly that the Apple II package
   A attracts most of the world's trade
   B is more versatile than other computers
   C is most preferred throughout the world
   D comes from a large international company

5. Which one of the following is closest in meaning to 'compatible'?
   A Able to integrate with the system
   B Adjustable to suit any conditions
   C Appropriate to any computer programme
   D Attractive to personal users in particular

6. The features stressed to sell the Apple IIe package include all the following *EXCEPT*
   A large data-storage
   B extendable capacity
   C perfect clarity
   D easy print-out

7. The popularity of Apple IIe as a professional computer is attributable to all the following features, among others, *EXCEPT* its
   A size of keyboard
   B universal hardware
   C extensive memory
   D choice of printers

Questions based on the third section

8. The great advantage claimed for 'disk drive' in use is that it finds information in *two* ways:
   1. mechanically
   2. efficiently
   3. quickly
   4. effortlessly

   A 1 and 2 only
   B 1 and 4 only
   C 2 and 3 only
   D 3 and 4 only

9. It is claimed that the qualities of the Apple disk-based system make it 'standard for business' *and*

A useful in building up data-files
B more up-to-date than all other computers
C economical in its use of programmers
D superior to cassettes and micro-drives

Questions based on the fourth section

10. Which one of the following words is closest in meaning to 'software'?
    A Programs
    B Disk-drive
    C Micro-drive
    D Cassettes

11. In praising its applications within the Home, the advertisement says that purchasing the Apple IIe system
    A offers opportunities to acquire additional equipment on good terms
    B provides a number of discounts on games and educational programs
    C allows essential additions to be made in very easy stages
    D affords everyone the chance to improve their own financial position

12. This section details some of the ways in which the Apple IIe system can
    A use data
    B design programs
    C increase intelligence
    D provide ideas

Questions based on the fifth section

13. The advertisement suggests that Prestel (large data-bank) facilities are available to purchasers of the Apple IIe system by
    A acquiring a new monitor to provide a read-out
    B buying additional equipment on more favourable terms than usual
    C using a special card which locks into the system
    D writing new programs to link up with national networks

14. All the following are examples of new formations of words or common words taken over by the computing industry and given specialised meanings *EXCEPT*
    A 'to access'
    B 'voucher'
    C 'closed user'
    D 'download'

Questions based on the sixth section

15. The opening sentence to this section skilfully gives the impression it is assumed that you
    A are a very intelligent person
    B have always wanted a computer
    C have decided to buy the package
    D are anxious to know much more

16. Which one of the following is closest in meaning to 'basics'?
    A Skills
    B Languages
    C Programs
    D Fundamentals

17. 'BASIC' is printed in capital letters because it refers to a
    A word that has been used a few lines earlier
    B set of technical operating instructions for the computer system
    C system of analysing data available in the computer's memory
    D word formed from the initial letters of other words

18. The words 'or less' added to the price indicate that
    A by using the vouchers it will work out cheaper
    B the manufacturers are about to announce price reductions
    C by shopping around it may be found cheaper
    D the figure includes all the optional extras mentioned

Questions based on the whole advertisement

19. All the following superlative qualities are claimed for the Apple IIe system *EXCEPT* that it
    A is the most popular of professional systems
    B has the widest range of software anywhere
    C can make use of the best programs available
    D is the most reliable and versatile of all computers

20. The advantages claimed for choosing the Apple IIe system, include all the following *EXCEPT*
    A initial low purchase costs
    B a wide range of applications
    C easy access to data
    D a chance of professional training

Development

Written work

1. Plan carefully and produce an advertisement to be printed in a Sunday colour supplement for a product you already own or would very much

like to buy. (Make sure you present its qualities attractively and that your advertisement is skilfully directed at the kind of audience you wish to reach.)

2. Write a letter to the company producing this advertisement *either* to ask for further information about their product (mentioning specific things you wish to know) *or* expressing your disappointment with a computer system you already own.

Oral work

Plan a well-structured discussion, with a chairman and speakers in favour and speakers against, on the beneficial effects the use of computers will have on the lives of your generation.

Further activities

Invite a computer expert (perhaps a member of your own school or college staff) to talk to your group about the ways computers could help you in the study of English. (Prepare in advance some interesting questions to raise: *e.g.* 'Does the computer have any value for us in our study of literature?')

Exploration 3

Read the following passage very carefully; then answer the questions which follow. *DO NOT GUESS.*

Strange Pets

One bright spring morning in 1976, Mrs Poppy Hull, an accountant, was strolling to work down Chertsey Road in Woking, Surrey. She felt what she thought was a pair of arms on her shoulders. Mrs Hull turned and saw that it was a lion. She collapsed. The lion stood over her until its owner arrived at the scene.   5

The lion's name was Shane and he was the fourteen-stone plaything of Mr Ronald Voice, who worked for a taxi company in Woking and kept his pet in an old double-decker bus. Mr Voice had been playing with the lion in his back garden just before the event occurred. It was not clear why it had approached Mrs Hull, unless it was because she 10
was wearing a leopard-skin coat.

As it happened, Mrs Hull was shaken but unhurt. Shane was quite harmless. The incident merely illustrates the alarm some pets may inspire. Lions, cheetahs, pythons and tarantulas are among the more obviously perilous creatures. But nature is red in tooth and claw, and 15
practically any creature may turn nasty. Reports of savage assaults flood in almost daily from around the world. Consider the following from the summer and autumn of 1982.

Kangaroo Punch (Australia): As Mr Danny Pocock, 59, a train driver, walked to work near Wycheproof, 175 miles north west of 20
Melbourne, a rogue red kangaroo sprang from nowhere and felled him with a series of expert punches. Mr Pocock described his ordeal as 'terrifying; he went up like a boxer and hit me with an almighty thump. He knocked me down three times altogether . . . and I lost all three rounds.'   25

Hamster Horror – Superhamster Feared screamed the headlines. At Burnt Oak, hamsters were taking over. Some terrified residents had to be moved from their homes as hordes of these small, normally timorous rodents infested the council estate at Hook Walk. Hamster shields were set up to protect houses, especially around television aerial 30
lines which the animals used as routes up walls and into bedrooms. The council was besieged with complaints.

Hamsters were first introduced into Britain as pets in the 1930s; it was thought that those of Burnt Oak were descended from the normal species but had somehow escaped captivity and gone wild, thriving in 35
rubbish bins, adapting to the harsh English winter. The Ministry of Agriculture was consulted and a number of poisons were tried – all

without success. Experts feared that the hamsters' ability to resist both
poisons and cold weather showed that they were on their way to
becoming superhamsters. Unchecked, they could spread over the rest   40
of the country, disturbing the food chain and posing serious problems
for agriculture.

Barnet Council ordered an all-out offensive. Officials came in
gumboots, armed to the teeth with traps and bait. But the hamsters
were too quick for them; not one of the furry beasts was caught after the   45
campaign began. Zoologists blamed the council's methods: tractor
mowers had been used to clear overgrown gardens, driving the
hamsters underground. One expert quoted in the *Hendon Times* said,
'Barnet Council really don't know much about the habits of hamsters
at all – hamsters burrow several feet down.'   50

Perhaps the hamsters had moved on to improve their stock
elsewhere. Or perhaps they still lurk in secret burrows beneath Burnt
Oak, waiting, waiting . . .

1. The writer mentions that Mrs Poppy Hull was 'an accountant' (line 1)
   presumably to show that she
   A was a responsible person
   B could add up figures
   C could use her imagination
   D worked in an office

2. Mrs Hull 'collapsed' (line 4) most probably because
   A the lion was heavy
   B she suffered a heart-attack
   C she was totally shocked
   D the lion looked fierce

3. Which one of the following words means 'plaything' as it is used in
   line 6?
   A Pet
   B Toy
   C Love
   D Fad

4. All the following facts are certain about Mr Ronald Voice *EXCEPT* that
   he
   A drove a taxi
   B kept a strange pet
   C had a garden
   D owned an old bus

5. Which one of the following is closest in meaning to 'As it happened' as used in line 12?
   A 'As strange as it seemed'
   B 'As a matter of fact'
   C 'As luck would have it'
   D 'As sure as houses'

6. 'Shane was quite harmless (lines 12–13) means that Shane
   A would never attack anyone
   B seemed almost human
   C enjoyed a good joke
   D would never frighten anyone

7. 'Lions, cheetahs, pythons and tarantulas' (line 14) are given as examples of creatures that are
   A frightening
   B exotic
   C savage
   D dangerous

8. The idiomatic expression 'red in tooth and claw' (line 15) means
   A bloodthirsty
   B savage
   C spiteful
   D murderous

9. The examples 'from the summer and autumn of 1982' (lines 17–18) the reader is invited to consider are meant to show that
   A odd events happen world-wide
   B assaults are an everyday happening
   C any creature can become ill-natured
   D pets can revert to nature

10. In which *two* of the following respects did Mr Danny Pocock (line 19) and Mrs Poppy Hull (line 1) resemble each other?
    1. Both lived in the suburbs of a large town.
    2. Both were terrified by what happened to them.
    3. Both encountered strange experiences on the way to work.
    4. Both were attacked by very dangerous animals.

    A 1 and 2 only
    B 1 and 4 only
    C 2 and 3 only
    D 3 and 4 only

11. It is clear from the account of Mr Pocock's encounter with the fighting kangaroo that he

    A was a quiet man
    B could look after himself
    C was a skilled fighter
    D tried to defend himself

12. A 'Superhamster' (line 26) is a species of hamster which can survive harsh weather conditions and which
    A has become immune to normal pest controls
    B sets out to harass its former owners
    C has developed into a wild and dangerous creature
    D grows and grows to an enormous size

13. Which one of the following is closest in meaning to *timorous* as used in line 29?
    A Extremely gentle
    B Easily frightened
    C Entirely harmless
    D Especially lovable

14. The hamster attack at Burnt Oak led to all the following *EXCEPT*
    A houses being evacuated
    B the council being criticised
    C the residents being terrified
    D television aerials being cut

15. The hamsters which became such a menace at Burnt Oak were all the following *EXCEPT*
    A creatures descended from domestic animals
    B survivors adapted to living rough
    C species introduced accidentally from abroad
    D pets escaped from their owners

16. The spread of Superhamsters country-wide would disturb the food-chain and create serious difficulties for
    A ecologists
    B farmers
    C gardeners
    D biologists

17. Which one of the following is equivalent to 'armed to the teeth' (line 44)? Armed
    A from top to toe
    B here and there
    C inside and out
    D back to front

18. The hamsters avoided capture by the officials by
    A running fast
    B burrowing deep
    C abandoning habitats
    D using cunning

19. The three dots at the end of the passage are intended to imply
    A doubt
    B humour
    C menace
    D excitement

20. The passage as a whole is mainly about
    A animals which behave suddenly out of character
    B threats to the supremacy of man
    C pets which become wild with frustration
    D disasters arising from man's attitude to animals

Development

Further reading

1. Rudyard Kipling, *Jungle Book* and *Second Jungle Book*, 1894–95 (now available in Macmillan Children's Books).
   The stories of Mowgli, the boy found and raised by wolves in the jungle who became friendly with Baboo the bear and Bagheera the panther and finally killed Shere Khan, the tiger, are classics about man's relationships with animals.
       Kipling's *Just So Stories*, 1902 (now available in Macmillan Children's Books), are beast fables which tell how the camel got his hump and the rhinoceros his folded skin.
2. Joy Adamson, *Born Free*, Collins paperbacks, 1973.
   This is a series of accounts of the way the writer raised a lioness from a cub and of the close relationship which grew up between them.
3. T. S. Eliot, *Old Possum's Book of Practical Cats*, Faber and Faber, 1939.
   Old Possum was a name given to the poet T. S. Eliot by another famous poet, Ezra Pound. Macavity is the mystery cat who has strangely disappeared whenever a 'crime' has been discovered, but there are others in the book which you will soon recognise from the pets you have known.

Written (and project) work

1. Imagine that you are your favourite pet. Give an account of life as it appears through your pet's eyes.
2. What do you consider the strangest animal in the world? Find out all you can about it and then describe its appearance, its habitat, its way of living, and its relationship with human beings, as if you are making an entry in a children's encyclopaedia.

Exploration 4

Read the following passage very carefully; then answer the questions which follow. *DO NOT GUESS.*

The Wedding

A sprinkling of girls in gay hats from Miriam's place of business appeared in church, great nudgers all of them, but only two came on afterwards to the house. Mrs Punt brought her son with his ever-widening mind – it was his first wedding; and a Larkins uncle, a Mr Voules, a licensed victualler, very kindly drove over in a high-hung dogcart from Sommershill with a plump, well-dressed wife, to give the bride away. One or two total strangers drifted into the church and sat down observantly in distant seats.

This sprinkling of people seemed only to enhance the cool brown emptiness of the church, the rows and rows of empty pews, disengaged prayer-books, and abandoned hassocks. It had the effect of a preposterous misfit. Johnson consulted with a thin-legged, short-skirted verger about the disposition of the party. The officiating clergy appeared distantly in the doorway of the vestry putting on his surplice, and relapsed into a contemplative cheek-scratching that was manifestly habitual. Before the bride arrived, Mr Polly's sense of the church found an outlet in whispered criticisms of ecclesiastical architecture with Johnson. 'Early Norman arches, eh?' he said, 'or Perpendicular.'

'Can't say,' said Johnson.

'Telessated pavements all right.'

'It's well laid anyhow.'

'Can't say I admire the altar. Scrappy rather with those flowers.

He coughed behind his hand and cleared his throat. At the back of his mind he was speculating whether flight at this eleventh hour would be criminal or merely reprehensible bad taste. A murmur from the nudgers announced the arrival of the bridal party.

The little procession from a remote door became one of the enduring memories of Mr Polly's life. The verger had bustled to meet it and arrange it according to tradition and morality. In spite of Mrs Larkins' impassioned 'Don't take her from me yet!' he made Miriam go first with Mr Voules, the bridesmaids followed, and then himself, hopelessly unable to disentangle himself from the whispering maternal anguish of Mrs Larkins. Mrs Voules, a compact, rounded woman with a square, expressionless face, imperturbable dignity, and a dress of considerable fashion, completed the procession.

Mr Polly's eyes fell first upon the bride; the sight of her filled him

with a curious stir of emotion. Alarm, desire, affection, respect – and a
queer element of reluctant dislike, all played their part in that complex
eddy.

*   *   *   *   *   *

The verger's hand pushed at him from behind. Someone was driv-   40
ing Miriam towards the altar rail and the clergyman. 'We're in for it,'
said Mr Polly to her sympathetically. 'Where? Here? Right O.'

He was interested for a moment or so in something indescribably
habitual in the clergyman's pose. What a lot of weddings he must have
seen! Sick he must be of them!   45
'Don't let your attention wander,' said the eye.[1]
'Got the ring?' whispered Johnson.
'Pawned it yesterday,' answered Mr Polly with an attempt at
lightness, and then had a dreadful moment under that pitiless scrutiny
while he felt in the wrong waistcoat pocket.   50
The officiating clergy sighed deeply, began, and married them
wearily and without any hitch.
'D'bloved we gath'd gether sighto Gard 'n face this con'gation join
gather Man Wom Ho Matmony whichis on'bl state stooted by Gard in
times mans in'cency . . .'   55
Mr Polly's thoughts wandered wide and far, and once again
something like a cold hand touched his heart, and he saw a sweet face in
sunshine under the shadow of trees.
Someone was nudging him. It was Johnson's finger diverting his
eyes to the crucial place in the prayer-book to which they had come.   60
'Wiltou lover, cumfer, oner keeper sickness and health . . .'
'*Say, "I will".*'
Mr Polly moistened his lips. 'I will,' he said hoarsely.
Miriam nearly inaudible, answered some similar demand.
Then the clergyman said: 'Who gi's Wom mad't this man?'   65
'Well, *I'm* doing that,' said Mr Voules in a refreshingly full voice and
looking round the church.
'Pete arf me,' said the clergyman to Mr Polly. 'Take thee Mirum
wed wife –.'
'Take thee Mi'm wed' wife,' said Mr Polly.   70
'Have hold this day ford.'
'Have hold this day ford.'
'Betworse, richypoo'.'
'Bet worse, richypoo' . . . .'
Then came Miriam's turn.   75
'Lego hands,' said the clergyman, 'gothering? No! On book. So!
Here! Pete arf me "Wis ring Ivy wed".'

---

1. *'The eye' was Mr Voules who was watching Mr Polly very closely indeed.*

'Wis ring Ivy wed –'

So it went on, blurred and hurried, like the momentary vision of a very beautiful thing seen through the smoke of a passing train . . .   80

'Now, my boy,' said Mr Voules at last, gripping Mr Polly's elbow tightly, 'you've got to sign the registry and there you are! Done!'

Before him stood Miriam, a little stiffly, the hat with a slight rake across her forehead, and a kind of questioning hesitation in her face. Mr Voules urged him past her.   85

It was astounding. She was his wife!

And for some reason Miriam and Mrs Larkin were sobbing, and Annie was looking very grave. Hadn't they after all wanted him to marry her? Because if that was the case –!

1. All the girls described in the first sentence were all the following *EXCEPT*
   - **A** dressed up for the occasion
   - **B** interested in what was happening
   - **C** invited to the reception later
   - **D** acquainted with the bride through work

2. 'A licensed victualler' (line 5) would have run a
   - **A** pub
   - **B** restaurant
   - **C** hotel
   - **D** club

3. 'Enhance' (line 9) means
   - **A** intensify
   - **B** symbolise
   - **C** offset
   - **D** dominate

4. All the following had arrived at the church before the best man consulted the verger (lines 12–13) *EXCEPT*
   - **A** the bridegroom
   - **B** Mrs Voules
   - **C** Mrs Punt
   - **D** the bride

5. The best man consulted the verger (lines 12–13) in order to find out
   - **A** who would be coming
   - **B** why the church was empty
   - **C** when the service would start
   - **D** where everyone should sit

6. A 'verger' (line 13) is a person in church who
   A officiates at weddings
   B looks after its interior
   C is responsible for services
   D plays the organ

7. 'Norman arches' (line 18) in shape are
   A square
   B rectangular
   C semicircular
   D pointed

8. When Mr Polly said 'Telessated pavements all right' (line 20) he was referring to the
   A altar
   B bricks
   C arches
   D floor

9. 'At the back of his mind' (lines 23–24) Mr Polly was speculating what view would be taken of his
   A coughing loudly
   B changing his mind
   C running away
   D altering the date

10. Which one of the following would certainly have been among the 'bridal party' (line 26)?
    A the verger
    B Mr Voules
    C Mrs Larkin
    D the vicar

11. When 'Mr Polly's eyes fell first upon the bride' (line 36) he felt all the following *EXCEPT*
    A fear
    B longing
    C fondness
    D hate

12. To what does 'that complex eddy' (lines 38–39) refer?
    A The disturbance caused by Mrs Larkins
    B The pushing behind Mr Polly's back
    C The state of Mr Polly's feelings
    D The procession in the aisle

13. Mr Polly's remark, 'We're in for it' (line 41), shows mainly that he had
    A   forgotten where to stand
    B   resented being pushed forward
    C   abandoned his earlier idea
    D   decided to look cheerful

14. 'Pawned it yesterday' (line 48) is a remark which showed Mr Polly was trying hard to
    A   distract attention
    B   be humorous
    C   worry everyone
    D   seem difficult

15. 'The officiating clergy' (line 51) seemed rather
    A   bored
    B   exhausted
    C   remote
    D   annoyed

16. The way the officiating clergy recited the words of the marriage service is best described as
    A   inaudible
    B   monotonous
    C   mechanical
    D   inexplicable

17. The comparison of the wedding service with the momentary vision of a very beautiful thing seen through the smoke of a passing train (lines 79–80) conveys its speed and its
    A   muddle
    B   indistinctness
    C   irregularity
    D   greyness

18. Mr Voules remarks 'Now my boy . . . . Done!' (lines 81–82) contains one glaring example of
    A   a misused word
    B   an ungrammatical construction
    C   an unfinished sentence
    D   a wrong tense

19. All the following remarks might have been possible ways for Mr Polly to end his final sentence *EXCEPT*
    A   . . . he wished he had known earlier
    B   . . . there was still time to change
    C   . . . they should have said so before
    D   . . . he would have left much earlier

20. In this account of a wedding the emphasis is placed mainly on
    A fear
    B sarcasm
    C ignorance
    D humour

Development

Written work

1. Give an account of a wedding (or some other major family gathering) you went to recently; try to make it a lively description intended to reveal your own attitude to a general reader. (If you decide to make it humorous, control your writing very carefully to let the humour work subtly on the reader.)

2. What qualities would you look for in someone you might marry in the future? Try to match these qualities against the picture you have of yourself to show why you would hope to find them in your future partner.

Project work

Try to find out as much as you can about marriage customs in other parts of the world. Then give an account of what you have discovered about the customs in *at least one other country.*

Further reading

Margaret Mead, *Coming of Age in Samoa*, 1928.
                   Growing Up in New Guinea, 1930.
(Both published in Pelican editions by Penguin Books)
These two very well-presented books about social customs and the life and relationships of a community in Polynesia have become classics of their kind. They contain descriptions of the way young people fall in love and marry in a society with its own strict patterns of behaviour.

Exploration 5

The following is an advertisement for a short holiday in France; it is taken from a holidays brochure aimed at school parties.

Read it carefully; then answer the questions which follow. *DO NOT GUESS*. (NB. There are 22 questions based on this passage.)

A Taste of France

Two days mini tour to Picardy with one night at our hotel from School to School by British Coach

Section One

A new mini-tour for 8–11 year olds

An ideal introduction to France for pupils just starting to learn French.

The Aims of the Visit

First and foremost, 'A Taste of France' aims to **stimulate the pupils' natural curiosity** concerning France and the French and thereby **increase their motivation** to learn the language. Most young children display an inherent enthusiasm to learn a foreign language. But so often, as the process of language learning seems to become progressively harder, the initial excitement fades through lack of motivation. 'A Taste of France' is intended to bring practical reality into classroom theory from the very outset of language learning. Pupils will actually see 'la mairie', 'le bureau de poste', 'l'église', 'la boulangerie', 'la boucherie' and other shops they are learning about at school. The fictional French family in the school textbook materialises into the real-life hotel proprietors, Monsieur and Madame Duflos with their three children.

In short, real people using real French as a natural means of communication.

Section Two

What advantages has 'A Taste of France' over the traditional day-trip to France?

Day-trips to Boulogne, Calais and even Dieppe have long been the traditional way to introduce schoolchildren to France. So many thousands of British people are in fact now pouring into these Channel ports, that they are fast in danger of losing their 'French flavour'.

'A Taste of France' on the other hand has many advantages to offer.

Less fatigue – especially significant when dealing with younger children. The very long journey time of a day trip can result in the crowded day becoming a nightmare of confused impressions overlaid by utter exhaustion.

A chance to explore France – through the availability of your own coach which fetches your party from school, crosses the Channel with you, stays with you throughout your visit and returns you to the school gates.

The opportunity to sample French food in a French environment. A carefully chosen evening meal in the hotel and the traditional French breakfast give every child the possibility of tasting the renowned French cuisine, without the dangers of protracted homesickness curbing appetites.

An overnight stay in a French hotel, full of French signs and notices and all the details that seem so different from home:- the cabinet de toilette of wash basin and bidet; shutters not curtains; bolsters not pillows; to name just a few.

Enough time to settle to the first stages of environmental study work: reading and recognising basic signs and shop names, absorbing the atmosphere of a genuinely French community without the jarring note introduced by 'fish and chip shops' or 'English Tea' so prevalent in the ports themselves.

Section Three

Your Centre

A mere 5 kilometres south of Boulogne, **Equihen Plage** is nonetheless a self-contained village with a separate identity. Many of the 3,000 inhabitants are fishermen keeping their boats at the nearby port of Boulogne, while their families fish the mussels and other seafoods washed up along their even coastline. A short walk (400 metres) from the hotel is a sandy beach confined by cliffs. Rock pools abound and at low tide, under the supervision of our hotelier, parties may themselves fish for the crab and 'wild' mussels to be caught there. In contrast to these 'moules sauvages', our parties may visit the 'Parc à Moules' (mussel breeding grounds) seven kilometres away (a guided tour lasts approximately one hour). Here they will appreciate that sea-food is big business – and will learn never to eat any when there is not an 'R' in the month!

Safety First must be a prime consideration of party leaders taking young children abroad. We have chosen Equihen for 'A Taste of France' for that very reason. A compact town centre that epitomises 'typical' French village life will give children a sense of identity in this undoubtedly foreign environment in a very short space of time.

The main square, 'la Place de Ménerville', is 200 metres from our hotel. In the heart of the little town, we find here the Town Hall and Post Office, a Tabac (also selling papers and souvenirs), a Boulangerie- Patisserie, a Charcuterie, a hardware shop and a café-bar.

Leading from the main square to the beach is 'la rue de l'Abbaye Coppin' where we find the Boucherie, the Pharmacie, the bank, the 'Marchand de légumes', bars and restaurants.

Cottage Industry

This long street offers much of interest to the young visitor. Children should look out for the home-made price boards outside many of the houses, advertising for sale the fresh shrimps, crabs, mussels and fish caught by the family. Cottage industry indeed. Equihen was almost totally destroyed during the last war. Nearby all the inhabitants lost their houses and were forced to shelter in upturned boats. On a sand dune overlooking the bay the children will be intrigued to see one of these unique little homes: a cottage made out of a fishing boat, with portholes for windows and a chimney built on to the stern.

Napoleon's Fort

Three short kilometres north of Equihen is the busy seaside resort of **Le Portel**. During the encampment of Napoleon's Grande Armée at Boulogne, between 1800 and 1805, the French commander decided to build a fort from which to launch his invasion of England. The ruins of his Fort de l'Heurt, built in 1803, can be reached on foot at low tide, but are surely most impressive viewed from the shore with the waves washing round the foundations of rock.

The market is held twice a week at Le Portel: on Tuesdays and Fridays between 8 a.m. and 12 noon. An indoor swimming pool (open most evenings) offers our parties an opportunity to relax from their concentrated studies.

Section Four

Your Hotel

The **Hôtel la Terrasse** is a simple, unpretentious family hotel, owned and run by the Duflos family. All rooms have either an enclosed cabinet de toilette or a wash basin. Shower and toilet facilities are on the landings. Pupils will be accommodated in rooms for three or four. As this hotel was furnished for families, nearly every bedroom contains a double bed, with one or two single beds; some of the children will therefore be expected to share a double bed.

Our parties will have the hotel to themselves. The bar will be closed to outside clients and in it the children will find flipper machines and two 'babyfoot' tables. As well as the restaurant, party leaders will have exclusive use of the large 'recreation room' for their project work, discussions, or even a disco if they so wish.

Section Five

Your Itinerary

Tour FR46

Departure from Dover, Eastern Docks on the midday ferry. On arrival at Boulogne, parties will immediately transfer to Equihen.

After settling into the hotel, pupils begin their studies by exploring Equihen with our Tour Quiz. *Please note: The market is held in Equihen on Thursday afternoons.* The remainder of the afternoon will be spent with the Schools Abroad 'Hotel Assignment' – designed to help the children recognise all the different room functions, basic instructions and notices. Before dinner there will be time for follow-up work and an exchange of ideas and first impressions.

Dinner will consist of home-made soup and a main dish followed by dessert. Free time after dinner may be spent on either further work (based on the Schools Abroad workbook 'Project France') or relaxation, as party leaders choose.

On the morning of Day 2, party leaders have a choice of activities for their group; we would recommend:

Visit 1: The Parc à Moules at Wimereux.

Visit 2: The pottery at Desvres (entrance fee 8F per person).

Visit 3: A 2-hour guided tour of Boulogne Old Town *or* the port of Boulogne (180F for the guide).

Visit 4: The unloading of the fishing catch in Boulogne harbour, accompanied by your hotelier, himself a former fish wholesaler.

Visit 5: The hypermarket at Boulogne.

Visit 6: Free time in Le Portel.

There are, of course, several other options open to party leaders, made possible by the availability of your own coach. Our office staff will be pleased to discuss these at your convenience. We would, however, ask for final details of excursion choices twelve weeks before your departure, so that we may make the necessary arrangements.

After a packed lunch, provided by the hotel, there is free time for shopping before check-in at the ferry terminal at 15.00 hours.

The return crossing will be made on the 16.00 hours ferry, arriving at Dover at approximately 16.40 hours, local time.

---

1. The 'headlines' to the advertisement promise all the following *EXCEPT*
    A no coach changes on the way
    B a stay overnight in a hotel
    C a short trip round part of France
    D no involvement with foreign people

Section One

2. The mini-tour aims to do all the following *EXCEPT*
    A encourage the desire to find out more
    B give the chance to learn a foreign language
    C reinforce what children are learning in school
    D show a foreign language actually being used

3. This section suggests that the enthusiasm of children starting to learn a foreign language often dies away because they
    A become bored in school
    B find the work too hard
    C see little point in it
    D think their textbooks are silly

4. Which one of the following words is closest in meaning to 'inherent' as used in the phrase 'an inherent enthusiasm to learn a foreign language'?
   A Natural
   B Eager
   C Deep
   D Obvious

Section Two

5. 'The traditional day-trip to France' is presented as having all the following disadvantages *EXCEPT* that it is
   A confusing in the impressions it leaves on children
   B uncharacteristic of the authentic taste of France itself
   C unable to let the children meet French people
   D tiring because of the time the journey takes

6. In the paragraph headed **Less Fatigue**, all the following words are intended to add to the black picture of the day-trip *EXCEPT*
   A significant
   B crowded
   C confused
   D utter

7. According to this section, British children might not like French food because
   A it is far too rich to be eaten in the evening
   B being away from home for a long time puts them off eating
   C the hotel menus and strange breakfasts need some getting used to
   D the exhaustion caused by the long journey gives them travel-sickness

8. The advantages of the mini-tour advertised over the traditional day-trip to France are given as all the following *EXCEPT*
   A the journey is easier and less tiring
   B there is more contact with the French themselves
   C the hotel will demonstrate the language being used
   D there is more food the children will appreciate

Section Three

9. Which *two* of the following are major sources of employment to the villagers in Equihen Plage?
   1. Hotel-keeping
   2. Catching fish
   3. Beach-combing
   4. Sea-food farming

A 1 and 2 only
B 1 and 3 only
C 2 and 4 only
D 3 and 4 only

10. The main feature of Equihen claimed to ensure its safety as a centre for
    schoolchildren is its
    A compactness
    B diversity
    C environment
    D typicalness

11. The major feature of a 'cottage industry' is that it
    A produces fresh products for the public
    B is carried on from the home
    C can advertise its goods very simply
    D has low overheads and high productivity

12. Which one of the following words is closest in meaning to 'intrigued' as
    used in the second paragraph under the heading **Cottage Industry** in
    this section?
    A Puzzled
    B Astonished
    C Amused
    D Fascinated

13. **Napoleon's Fort** is introduced as a possible attraction to school parties
    for all the following reasons *EXCEPT* that it
    A has fallen into ruins
    B is of historical importance
    C is impressive in appearance
    D lies near a beach

14. **Le Portel** offers all the following attractions *EXCEPT*
    A a historical site
    B a lot of shops
    C a rocky coastline
    D a chance to relax

Section Four

15. Which one of the following means 'unpretentious'?
    A Not very comfortable
    B Not charging too much
    C Not too sham
    D Not claiming too much

16. All the rooms in the **Hôtel la Terrasse** contain
    A a shower
    B a wash-basin
    C a double-bed
    D a toilet

17. The fact that 'our parties will have the hotel to themselves' will have
    which *one* of the following effects?
    A They can do as they like.
    B They will meet few local people.
    C They will feel immediately at home.
    D They can plan their own menus.

Section Five

18. The Tour Quiz is likely to contain questions on
    A the outward journey
    B personal opinions
    C local features
    D the hotel's accommodation

19. The 'Hotel Assignment' is intended mainly to encourage the under-
    standing of
    A the safety regulations to be followed
    B the French language in current use
    C the differences between English and French hotels
    D the opportunities available for work and leisure

20. According to earlier claims in the advertisement, the evening meal
    (dinner) will
    A help to offset any feeling of homesickness
    B give an opportunity to sample French family cooking
    C provide an example of renowned French cuisine
    D consist of food all the children will like

21. The 'choice of activities' for the morning of Day 2 is possible mainly
    because
    A their cost is comparatively low
    B the coach is readily available
    C they lie on the way home
    D their planning is an easy matter

22. All the following are features of the return trip to Dover *EXCEPT*
    A a chance to make last-minute purchases
    B a meal provided by the hotel
    C a twenty-minute sea crossing
    D a wait at the ferry terminal

Development

Written work

1. Imagine that you are a teacher and took a school party on the holiday advertised; things went somewhat wrong and you decided to write a letter of complaint to the tour company. Set out the details of your complaints clearly, politely, but firmly.
2. Give an account of a school trip abroad which you enjoyed.
3. It is assumed by schools that it is important to learn a foreign language. Which foreign language do you think is the most important to learn? Give your reasons, with some examples, to justify your choice.

Activities

1. Invite two or three children from overseas to talk to your group or class about their impressions of your own country. Try to find out why they think it is important to learn your language. What do they find is most difficult about it?
2. From your study of an overseas country, plan an interesting four-day trip to it for a small school party. (You may present your plans in the form of an advertisement, if you wish, and may draw maps, include pictures, and use the native language to make your proposed trip seem attractive.)

Further reading

Find another advertisement from a travel brochure or a holiday programme. Read it carefully to see if it contains any unsupported claims, contradictions, and misleading information. (Look particularly for any words or phrases which 'slant' the writing to emphasise some attractive features and play down others; omissions are sometimes as significant as the facts included.)

Exploration 6

Read the following passage carefully; then answer the questions which follow. *DO NOT GUESS*.

The Hindenberg

By 1936 the Germans had completed the *Hindenberg* to join its sister ship *Graf Zeppelin*. With a length of rather more than 800 feet, she was the biggest airship ever built. Power came from four mighty Daimler diesel engines driving propellers in separate gondolas under the great gas-lifted hull. As with all airships, the gas was contained in a quantity   5
of separate bags, or cells. Today, those would be made completely gas-tight but in 1937 a slow seepage was expected and allowed for.

This brought with it the danger of fire, but designers had perfected the interior passenger quarters, with their 25 two-berth cabins, spacious dining-room, saloon and reading-room, so that there was   10
almost no risk of hydrogen entering. Smoking was confined to one absolutely safe room, with double-doors and an ingenious method of keeping its air pressure higher than elsewhere, so that no gas could possibly enter. Passengers could smoke freely here, though the cigarette-lighters were chained to tables to prevent the absent-minded   15
taking them to their bedrooms.

Elsewhere, in this ingenious, luxurious ship, was a baby grand piano, made of aluminium. On either side were promenade decks from which passengers could look out and down through big sloping windows.   20

The *Hindenberg* made a number of flights to the United States and to Brazil during 1936–37, and May 1937 brought yet another scheduled departure from Frankfurt to the American terminus at Lakehurst. Nothing could have been more routine; no German passenger airship or Zeppelin had yet crashed. From those first flights in 1910, many   25
thousands of people had been carried safely to their destinations.

Slowly she rose into Frankfurt's sky on the evening of 3 May. Her passenger accommodation was half empty (though it was almost fully booked for the return trip) and the 36 on board, with a standard crew, totalled 97. Estimated time of arrival at Lakehurst was 8 a.m. on the   30
6th, but very soon Captain Max Pruss realised that strong headwinds were going to upset the schedule.

It was already 15.30 on the 6th when *Hindenberg* passed over New York's Empire State Building – a regular practice, to advertise Germany and her great airship to the people below, and give   35
passengers an exciting, unfamiliar look at the city. However, what

interest there might have been in the arrival of another airship flight was diminished, rather than heightened, by its lateness. Apart from passengers' friends and relatives, few people were heading for Lakehurst. Hardly any of the press were turning out; one radio   40 company had sent a commentator, Herb Morrison, with a portable recorder.

Bad weather made Pruss delay his arrival still further, and it was not until 7.00 p.m. that he began his approach to the Lakehurst mooring-mast.   45

The first lines were dropped to the ground crew at 7.25 p.m. A slightly bored Herb Morrison began his commentary, unaware that it would become one of the most moving records of human anguish.

There was a flame, and Morrison's voice, abruptly kindling with it   50 to hysteria, sobbed, 'It's broken into flames; it's flashing, flashing, flashing terribly; it's bursting into flames!'

Those inside were the last to know, and to this day no one can be sure what caused that flame. Miraculously, with seven million cubic feet of incandescent hydrogen about them, only 36 died out of   55 *Hindenberg*'s airborne total of 97. Much credit for this must go to officers and men at Lakehurst, who risked death to lead shocked, hurt, passengers and crew out of the holocaust.

So ended the day of the passenger airship. The rest of the world, including Britain, which had been watching the Germans with   60 interest, gave up hope that these monsters of the sky would ever be safe and practical. There were undoubtedly other unspoken consider-ations, for no industry could die with such a small casualty list. The Germans withdrew the perfectly safe *Graf Zeppelin* in 1938, and in retrospect the reason is obvious. Zeppelins were not war machines.   65 Balloons continued, however, while the real hardware of fighters and bombers took over.

There remains the possible return of the airship for freight transportation. Independent of land or sea it can travel 'as the crow flies', which offers advantages. In the long term, the issue will be   70 decided by sheer economics, for a freight airship must make a profit if it is to survive – or even become a reality.

1. The *Hindenberg* and the *Graf Zeppelin* were airships
   A identical in every minute respect
   B intended to ply similar routes
   C built on the same model
   D designed to float side by side

2. Which one of the following words is closest in meaning to 'gondolas' as used in line 4?

A Cars
B Bags
C Cells
D Baskets

3. 'This' in line 3 refers to
   A the separate storage of gas
   B the slow leakage of gas
   C the hull filled with gas
   D the allowance made for the gas

4. 'Ingenious' (line 12) means
   A complex
   B skilful
   C careful
   D scientific

5. All the following were used to minimise the risk of an explosion on the Hindenberg *EXCEPT*
   A almost gas-proof living accommodation
   B a totally sealed smoking-room
   C a strict control of air-pressure
   D drastic cuts in cabin-accommodation

6. 'The cigarette-lighters were chained to tables (line 15) in order to stop passengers
   A smoking
   B causing fires
   C causing explosions
   D stealing

7. The baby grand piano was 'made of aluminium' (line 18) presumably in order to
   A improve its appearance
   B decrease its weight
   C decrease its cost
   D improve its tone

8. 'Promenade decks' (line 18) are decks made expressly for
   A sitting down
   B relaxing in deckchairs
   C admiring the view
   D strolling about

9. 'Scheduled' (line 22) means
   A timetabled
   B spectacular
   C expected
   D ordinary

10. Before 3 May 1937, German airships were known for all the following *EXCEPT* their
    A excellent record of safety
    B large numbers of passengers carried
    C regular schedule of flights
    D reliable times of arrival

11. The total number of people carried by the *Hindenberg* when it was full would have been about
    A 97
    B 133
    C 155
    D 196

12. Which *two* of the following were the reasons why the *Hindenberg* always passed over New York's Empire State Building?
    1. For propaganda purposes
    2. To attract the press
    3. To entertain the passengers
    4. For navigating purposes

    A 1 and 2 only
    B 1 and 4 only
    C 2 and 3 only
    D 3 and 4 only

13. 'Hardly any of the press were turning out' (line 40) to welcome the *Hindenberg* because it was late and
    A airship arrivals had become commonplace
    B radio companies employed few reporters
    C foreign nations had enough free advertising
    D people had seen it passing over

14. The lines 'dropped to the ground crew at 7.25 p.m.' (line 46) were used for
    A advertising
    B mooring
    C steering
    D descending

15. 'Kindling' (line 50) means becoming
    A excited
    B choked
    C overwhelmed
    D broken

16. Which one of the following is uncertain about the *Hindenberg* disaster?
   A How the survivors escaped
   B The number of dead
   C The cause of the flame
   D How the gas burnt

17. Which one of the following is closest in meaning to 'the holocaust' as used in line 58? The
   A dreadful tragedy
   B terrible accident
   C mass slaughter
   D twisted wreckage

18. The fact that there were 'undoubtedly other unspoken considerations' (lines 62–63) why the Germans halted the development of airships was clear because
   A the number of casualties had been small
   B the balloons had already proved their usefulness
   C the preparation for a world war had started
   D the designers turned their attention to aircraft

19. Which one of the following is closest in meaning to 'in retrospect' (lines 64–65)?
   A Looking back
   B In perspective
   C On consideration
   D Thinking hard

20. The element which will decide whether airships return or not will be
   A navigational
   B political
   C tactical
   D financial

Development

Further reading

1. Jules Verne, *Five Weeks in a Balloon*, 1863.
   An adventure story about Dr Fergusson and two companions who try to cross Africa from east to west in the days when ballooning was just beginning. Thunderstorms, winds, lions and hostile tribes present them with a few difficulties.
   (This story is published together with Jules Verne's story *Around the World in Eighty Days* in J. M. Dent's 'Everyman's Library' series.)
2. Albert Lamorisse, *The Red Balloon*, translated from the French by M. Barnes, Allen and Unwin, 1980.

Written work

1. Write an account for publication in a popular newspaper of the greatest disaster in history you can find? (You may imagine, if you wish, that you were an eye-witness.)
2. Argue the case for and against the re-introduction of airships for carrying both passengers and cargo.

Discussion

Hold a class 'Balloon Debate'. (Six members put forward their reasons why they should not be among the first to be pushed out of the basket of a balloon that must be lightened to avoid disaster for everyone. Why should they be saved in preference to everyone else? The six members may speak as themselves or adopt the roles of well-known politicians, pop-stars, broadcasters, inventors, scientists, artists, etc.)

Exploration 7

Read the following passage carefully; then answer the questions which follow. *DO NOT GUESS.*

Floods in Florence

The heaviest cultural blow was struck by the flood in 1966 at Florence and this aspect of Italy's disaster above all others caught the horrified imagination of the world. Cradle of the Italian Renaissance, a major shrine of Western civilisation, with its palaces, magnificent Romanesque buildings, and 40 museums housing many of the world's greatest art treasures, Florence was to suffer the fate of Venice – and worse.

On 4 November, the River Arno traversing the oldest part of the city burst its banks. Normally a man running can keep pace with the fastest flowing river, but on this day the Arno in a huge ungovernable flood surged forward at 40 miles an hour (a film made on the spot shows a car being hurled down the Via Formabuoni at just this speed). For several hours the torrent poured through the city spreading ever wider, flooding buildings and rising in places, including the Cathedral Square and the famous eleventh-century Baptistry, to over 15 feet. The best that anyone could do was to save a few possessions and escape drowning. Twenty-four hours later the deluge began to abate, leaving behind a massive residue of glutinous yellow mud, and in the following days it was possible to start surveying the damage. Final estimates showed 17 people dead, 45,000 homeless (a tenth of the population), 40,000 cars wrecked as well as 18,000 shops, including the workshops of some of the goldsmiths and leather-workers for which Florence was famous.

The loss and damage were enormous. Again, oil from burst tanks, and in some places naphtha, mixed with the flood and added to its destructiveness. Many famous buildings were swamped, among them the Medici Chapel, the San Firenzi Palace, the Casa di Dante, the Capella del Pazzi at Santa Croce and the church of Santa Maria Novella. Six hundred paintings by well-known masters were under water for hours when the basement of the famous Uffizi Gallery was flooded. Totally destroyed at the same time were 130,000 photographic negatives of Florentine art, many of them irreplaceable.

Elsewhere in the city there were other heavy casualties: the entire State Records of Tuscany from the fourteenth century to 1860, nineteenth-century newspaper files – a loss now making a detailed

history of the Risorgimento* impossible, Etruscan collections in the
Archaeological Museum, the musical scores of Scarlatti, the private
papers of Amerigo Vespucci (the Italian explorer who gave his name to
America) and the earliest painting in Western art, the 'Crucifixion' by   40
Cimabue (1240–1302).

Worst hit of all were the libraries. For days more than 6,000,000
volumes, a great many of them unique, lay submerged under water and
murky sludge in the State Archives and the vaults of the Biblioteca
Nazionale, the equivalent of the British Museum Library – a potential   45
loss which would have had a shattering effect on every aspect of future
study and research. At once, a massive international rescue operation
was set in motion, with experts from all over Europe coming to advise
and help. Even so, the restoration, wherever possible, of these works
and the paintings was to take years. Owing to the dissolving of the glue   50
used in bindings and size in the paper, many books when salvaged were
as solid as bricks. Each volume had to be cleaned, dried, treated with
chemicals to prevent fungus and the pages cautiously prised apart.
Finally, each volume had to be rebound.

Every job of restoration had to be done as soon as possible to avoid   55
rapid deterioration and speed was achieved by giving crash courses to
teams of students and then putting them under the supervision of a
single expert. All this caught the attention of the outside world, but
naturally the people involved in the 36,000 square miles of Italy that
had been devastated were more interested in obtaining credit to get on   60
their feet again. There had been damage in 800 municipalities; 22,000
farms and private homes had suffered; 50,000 animals had been lost,
thousands of tractors made useless. Total damage was estimated at
£575 million ($1,090 million). The death-toll in all Italy was 112.

In Florence, a fortnight after the disaster, the people were working   65
hard to succour the homeless, start business again and clean up their
beautiful city. They were not relying much on government help; they
knew official red tape too well. Enthusiasm bursting through his sober
prose, the London *Times* correspondent noted: 'Tuscan sturdiness has
risen above the ruin of the city's delicate grace.' He noticed an   70
interesting point: it was the 'beatniks', so criticised by their elders as
useless wasters, who were flinging themselves into relief work with the
most astonishing energy. 'Beatniks', he added, 'are better than
bureaucrats.'

A year later the people were back in their homes and at work again.   75
Museums, galleries and libraries had re-opened and it was said that:
'The golden city of the Renaissance glitters again.' But despite
intensive work on the river-bed and its banks, and the organisation of a

* The Liberation and Re-unification of Italian states in the nineteenth century

flood early-warning system, anxiety must remain. Asked what would
happen if it rained like *that* again, a city official replied: 'We must just   80
hope that it won't.'

1. The thing that 'above all others caught the horrified imagination of the
   world' (lines 1–2) was the fact that at Florence
   A the greatest art treasures were lost to civilisation
   B flood water rose higher than anywhere else
   C damage was much more extensive than elsewhere
   D the losses in other regions would be repeated

2. Florence is described as 'cradle of the Italian Renaissance' (line 3)
   because, in the writer's view, it was there that the Renaissance was
   A nurtured
   B perfected
   C established
   D invented

3. Which one of the following is closest in meaning to 'shrine' as used in
   line 4?
   A Place where hallowed objects are kept
   B Tomb where past relics are buried
   C Museum where art treasures are shown
   D Monument where pilgrims pay their respects

4. The disaster at Florence began with
   A the loss of many art treasures
   B the destruction of a nearby town
   C the path the river bed took
   D the river bursting its banks

5. The *three* factors which led to such widespread destruction were the
   river's volume and its
      1. huge speed
      2. change of course
      3. lack of control
      4. enormous depth

   A 1 and 2 only
   B 1 and 3 only
   C 2 and 4 only
   D 3 and 4 only

6. The failure of the banks to contain the River Arno led to all the following
   EXCEPT
   A risk to life
   B tremendous panic
   C widespread flooding
   D destruction of property

7. After the floods had gone down the immediate effect was that Florence seemed
   A emptied of its population
   B covered in sticky sludge
   C littered with dead and dying
   D full of collapsed buildings

8. 'Naphtha' (line 25) is a kind of
   A acid
   B sulphur
   C detergent
   D oil

9. According to the third paragraph (lines 24–33), the polluted water threatened all the following *EXCEPT*
   A photographic archives
   B celebrated paintings
   C historical houses
   D artists' studios

10. Which one of the following is closest in meaning to 'casualties' as used in line 34?
    A Injured people
    B Damaged objects
    C Threatened paintings
    D Catastrophic accidents

11. All the following items destroyed by the flood are said to be irreplaceable *EXCEPT*
    A state records covering about five centuries
    B newspapers from the nineteenth century
    C photographic records of works of art
    D personal diaries of the earliest explorer

12. The comparison between 'the Biblioteca Nazionale' and 'The British Museum Library' (lines 44–45) is intended to emphasise the Italian Library's
    A huge book stock
    B number of vaults
    C importance for research
    D unique archive collection

13. The 'rescue operation' (line 47) to help Florence's libraries consisted of all the following *EXCEPT*
    A giving advice
    B restoring books
    C using expertise
    D replacing documents

14. Damage to the books in Florence's libraries consisted of all the following *EXCEPT* that
    A bindings had fallen apart
    B paper was soaked right through
    C volumes were attacked by fungus
    D pages had stuck tightly together

15. 'Crash courses' (line 56) are courses
    A organised to use students' skills
    B designed to be led by experts
    C planned to meet an emergency
    D arranged to make temporary repairs

16. The majority of Italians in the parts of the country 'that had been devastated' (lines 59–60) were mainly interest in
    A recovering their livelihoods
    B draining their farms
    C mending their equipment
    D repairing the treasures

17. Which one of the following is closest in meaning to 'succour' as used in line 66?
    A Give shelter to
    B Help in distress
    C Track down quickly
    D Distribute relief to

18. In cleaning up 'their beautiful city' (line 66) the Florentines looked first of all to
    A their own efforts
    B state assistance
    C relief workers
    D their own officials

19. The *Times* correspondent was particularly impressed by the work of the
    A youthful tramps
    B adolescent anarchists
    C young drop-outs
    D teen-age drug-addicts

20. In the event of another similar flood, the writer concludes that Florence is
    A well protected
    B totally undefendable
    C completely doomed
    D still vulnerable

Development

Further reading

Read *Genesis*, chapters 6–8, in *The Bible* for an account of a world flood.
Then read the play, 'Noah's Flood', which is a dramatised re-working, often
with a humorous effect, of the Biblical account performed in Chester as long
ago as the fifteenth century. (You will find this play in a collection of
medieval plays edited by A. C. Cawley, *Everyman and Medieval Miracle
Plays*, Dent's Everyman's Library, second edition, 1957.)
NB. There was another play about Noah and his wife and sons written at
  Wakefield in the early part of the fifteenth century.

Project work

Find out from The Thames Water Authority (New River Head, Rosebery
Avenue, London, EC1R 4TP: 01-837-3300) what steps have been taken in
London to prevent flooding by the River Thames. Then draw a map
outlining their plans and give a full account of the measures they would take
in an emergency.

   You may wish to investigate, too, other plans taken to prevent flooding or
reduce its effects in your own district or country.

Exploration 8

Read the following passage very carefully; then answer the questions which follow. *DO NOT GUESS*. (NB. There are 25 questions set on this passage.)

Robots

At the time of writing there are 10,000 robot workers in Japanese factories, about half that number in the United States, some 3,000 in the Soviet Union, 713 in Britain and about 600 in France. Unquestionably, Japan leads the world in the field of automation and already its robots are posing problems: one mechanical monster has 5 gone berserk and killed a man in a Japanese car factory.

A robot is an apparently human automation; the term was coined as early as 1920, in a play called R.U.R. (Rossum's Universal Robots) written by the Czech writer Čapek. *Robota* means 'forced labour' in Czech, but since the machines have become a reality, safety advisers 10 have had to draw up guides on how to keep robots subservient. In June, 1982, the *Daily Telegraph* outlined some of the problems: 'Unlike other automated machinery, robots move about in unpredictable patterns. In a modern car works they look like evil ostriches, with necks and beaks making darting, stabbing actions as they wield welding 15 equipment, spitting sparks.'

Apprehensive *Guardian* readers were alarmed only two months later by a piece headlined: 'Robot Jailed'. It disclosed that a four-foot robot was hauled off to police cells when it was unable to give an account of itself as it strode, lights flashing, along the exclusive Beverley Drive in 20 Los Angeles. A policeman was called to the scene and, when the robot failed to respond to questioning, the suspect was taken down to the station in a police van.

A police spokesman said: 'The device was being operated by remote control, but the operator refused to come forward and identify 25 himself – so the robot is spending the night in the station.' He did not say whether the robot was being charged.

Of course, robots are not all bad: many are perfectly law-abiding. Indeed, the latest developments suggest that robot security guards will shortly be employed to protect business premises. Burglars will be 30 relieved to know that one thing the robots will not be programmed to do is to assault and pulverise. Once an intruder is cornered, the mechanical monsters will simply scream – very, very loudly. And as the terrified malefactor stands riveted to the ground with fright, the robot will summon the police by radio. 35

The potential of robots appears to be limitless. Already the Japanese factory of Fanuc, eighty miles west of Tokyo, is staffed by robots which make the parts for other robots. In this, the world's most advanced robot-manufacturing plant, up to a hundred robots are made each month. The factory runs twenty-four hours a day and has practically 40 dispensed with human intervention. So far, the work-force seems contented – there have been no strikes.

Will the robots eventually dispense with us altogether? The concept appears to belong to the realm of science fiction, and yet it is not as entirely fanciful as might be thought. According to a London 45 conference on computing, held in July, 1982, Japan is engaged in an all-out effort to construct machines that will be more intelligent than people. An electronic 'Pearl Harbour' was feared, spearheaded by machines that would be able to see, hear, talk, recognise individual human faces, and 'think'. 50

The robots are being developed by programmers known as 'knowledge engineers'. The moral question – 'Should it be allowed?' – is of no apparent concern. Christian notions about the immortality of the human soul do not coincide entirely with the precepts of the Shinto religion, where inert objects such as rocks and trees are credited with 55 powers of feeling.

But can robots ever truly be made to 'think'? The problem involves much complex discussion. Certainly, as far as measurable intelligence goes, the answer is yes. Computers have, for example, been success-fully programmed to play chess at a very high level, even competing 60 against each other in international events. The organiser of one such contest, quoted in the *Sunday Times*, declared, 'Computers are quite good at openings, which depend mainly on memory, and middle games. But they are very bad at end games. They often lose end games from a winning position. Overall, I would say computers are a bit 65 above the level of the weaker club players.'

To encourage computers to develop that killer instinct for the end game, much subsequent research has been undertaken. It is estimated that computers will be able to beat grandmasters by the end of the century – about the same time as Japan's incredibly sophisticated 70 talking robots will be at large.

1. 'Robot workers' (line 1) are
   A persons not very interested in their job
   B machines programmed to operate independently
   C persons who use modern methods of production
   D machines designed to eliminate human skills
   E persons not able to think very clearly

2. According to the first sentence (lines 1–3), which one of the following roughly represented Japan's lead numerically in robot workers over the total of all the other major countries mentioned?

A   576
B   687
C   867
D 5,657
E 5,687

3. Which one of the following expressions is closest in meaning to 'berserk' as used in line 6?
   A Madly aggressive
   B Totally insane
   C Utterly evil
   D Completely wild
   E Violently frenzied

4. The example of a mechanical monster which went berserk and killed a man (lines 5–6) is given mainly to show that robots
   A can have minds of their own
   B should be banned from factories
   C can finally take over the world
   D should be stopped from attacking workers
   E can easily get out of control

5. Which one of the following is closest in meaning to 'was coined' in line 7?
   A Was used
   B Became fashionable
   C Was suggested
   D Gained currency
   E Was invented

6. Use a dictionary if you need to, to say which one of the following is the reason Capek's play was called *R.U.R.* The title was
   A a homonym
   B an anagram
   C a palindrome
   D an acronym
   E a cryptogram

7. The explanation that '*Robota* means "forced labour" in Czech' (line 9) is given to stress the danger that robots
   A will one day destroy the world
   B stop people from working any harder
   C could make men their servants
   D have led to serious safety risks
   E will soon take over all production

8. The comparison between robots and ostriches in line 14 is intended to show that robots seem

A clumsy
B ridiculous
C gigantic
(D) dangerous
E funny

9. Which one of the following words means 'apprehensive' as used in line 17?
A Unbelieving
(B) Fearful
C Baffled
D Thoughtful
E Uncertain

10. Which one of the following means 'to give an account of itself' as used in lines 19–20?
A Control itself
B Defend itself
C Programme itself
D Believe itself
(E) Explain itself

11. The policeman took the robot 'down to the station' (lines 22–23) in a police van because
A robots had no right to be out walking
(B) it ignored what was said to it
C robots were potentially very dangerous creatures
D it refused to display any self-control
E robots had no knowledge of the law

12. The police statement given in lines 24–26 assumed that the robot was
A acting independently
B out of control
(C) obeying signals
D out of bounds
E being awkward

13. 'He did not say whether the robot was being charged' (lines 26–27) presumably because the police
A hoped the operator would come forward
B could not make up their minds
C managed to retain their sense of humour
(D) had no intention of taking action
E intended to prosecute the operator himself

14. Lines 7–27 suggest that robots were all the following *EXCEPT*
    A menacing
    B uncontrollable
    C wicked
    D uncommunicative
    E lawless

15. The fifth paragraph (lines 28–35) shows mainly that robots
    A could change their behaviour at will
    B preferred to co-operate with man
    C could help to maintain the law
    D preferred to assault and pulverise law-breakers
    E could destroy burglars with a noise

16. The effect of a robot's screaming at a malefactor would be to
    A drive him into a corner
    B frighten him to death
    C deter him from law-breaking
    D immobilise him through fear
    E deafen him with noise

17. 'The potential of robots appears to be limitless' (line 36) because they can do all the following *EXCEPT*
    A operate with little human supervision
    B work without going on strike
    C staff factories to make more robots
    D work right round the clock
    E reproduce themselves without man's help

18. The answer to the question, 'Will the robots dispense with us altogether?' (line 43), that the writer gave was
    A 'Only in the wildest imagination.'
    B 'The Japanese will bring it about.'
    C 'Never, because intelligence cannot be constructed.'
    D 'The Japanese will make thinking computers.'
    E 'Probably not in the immediate future.'

19. The 'all-out effort' (line 47) of the Japanese might well lead to machines which could do all the following *EXCEPT*
    A imitate human speech
    B recognise noises
    C distinguish faces
    D produce inventions
    E make out objects

20. The word 'think' in line 57 is in inverted commas because it
    A is used in a special sense
    B forms a kind of exclamation
    C is a summary of the paragraph
    D means really the exact opposite
    E is a quotation from a conference

21. The answer to the question 'But can robots ever truly be made to "think"?' (line 57) given by the writer is
    A 'Only in a limited sense.'
    B 'If they are correctly programmed.'
    C 'Only in some specialised games.'
    D 'If the complex problems are solved.'
    E 'Only when they measure intelligence.'

22. The problem computers face in playing chess is that they
    A can only follow their memories
    B lose interest in the game
    C begin well but finished badly
    D fail in international competitions
    E can only compete with weak opponents

23. Chess is considered a game in which robots will ultimately triumph because it relies largely on
    A random chance
    B measurable intelligence
    C sound research
    D killer instincts
    E good memory

24. Which one of the following is closest in meaning to 'sophisticated' as used in line 70?
    A Complex and intelligent
    B Ruthless and clever
    C Menacing and calculating
    D Refined and subtle
    E Complicated and up-to-date

25. According to the passage as a whole, robots would soon be able to do all the following *EXCEPT*
    A win chess tournaments
    B recognise human beings
    C guard business premises
    D produce motor cars
    E adopt religious ideas

Development

Further reading

1. Isaac Asimov, *Robot AL-76 Goes Astray*.
   In 1941 Asimov formulated the 'Three Laws of Robotics': (1) A robot may not injure a human being or through inaction allow a human being to come to harm; (2) A robot must obey the orders given to it by human beings except when such orders would conflict with the First Law; (3) A robot must protect its own existence as long as such protection does not conflict with the First and Second Laws. Robot AL-76 observes all three laws scrupulously. The characters, the situation, and the language of the story often seem to be a parody of the 'Western' with an eccentric shack-dweller (Randolph Payne), a shrewish wife (Mirandy), Sam Tobe of the Petersboro Branch of the United States Robot and Mechanical Man Corporation, Sheriff Saunders, Lank Jake, the Deputy, and the frightened farmers of Hannaford County, Virginia. The misunderstood robot stands firmly but forlornly at the centre of the narrative, like the innocent but maligned fugitive in a Western.
2. John Wyndham, *Compassion Circuit*.
   This is the story of Janet, who returns home after five days in hospital only to find a resident domestic nurse, Nurse James – who happens to be a robot. The sick woman is removed back to hospital where an operation completely changes her into a robot herself. George, her husband, is terrified . . .

[Both these stories are included in R. A. Banks (ed.), *Ten Science Fiction Stories*, Hodder and Stoughton, 1977], an anthology which contains some of the very best examples of Science Fiction and which traces the history of the genre from Plato to the present day.

Written work

1. Imagine that you are a robot which has 'gone astray' or even 'berserk' and has been arrested. (Think of a situation where your actions have had some serious (or humorous) consequences.) Write an account for the police describing and justifying what you have done.
2. Think of three situations in which robots could contribute to human happiness in the future. Describe these three situations and comment on the effect that the introduction of robots into them is likely to have on the lives of people.
3. Write a short Science Fiction story in which a robot plays the central role (It may be the hero or heroine, or the villain, or a reporter, or an alien, or a leader of a group, or a Dalek-type figure, etc.)

Exploration 9

Read the following passage very carefully; then answer the questions which follow. *DO NOT GUESS*.

A Little Sister's Nightmare

It could not have been long after midnight when I found myself awake, and so thoroughly awake, too. I did not feel the misty withdrawal or the drowsy approaches of sleep. I had apparently been reasoning, for some seconds, with admirable lucidity on the practical question: how had I come to wake up? The night was still. The ridiculous acorn-shaped   5
appendage to the blind-cord no longer flapped in its eddying elliptical movement. And what of that odious bluebottle fly? Doubtless it had crept into some corner, a fold in the valance, perhaps. I could not believe it was asleep. It might be scratching itself with one foot, in the way flies have.   10

It must have been someone knocking. My small sister slept in the next room. I remember her parting words, uttered in a voice that was half appeal, half command: 'Now, if I dream I'm being murdered I shall knock on the wall, and I shall expect you to come.' Of course, I reflected with uneasy amusement, my sister always had a lot to say at   15
bedtime. It was a recognised device; it gained time; it gave an effect of stately deliberation to her departure. It was, in fact, the exercise of a natural right. One could not be packed off to bed in the middle of a sentence. One would linger over embraces; one would adopt attitudes and poses too rich and noble for irreverent interruption; one would   20
drift into conversations and display a sudden interest. . . .

Tap-tap-tap-tap.

As I thought. Now what had put this silly idea into my sister's head? It was absurd that a child could dream of being murdered. It would not occur to her that there were such dreams. But perhaps someone had   25
suggested it – a servant whose mind was brimful of horrors. I myself had mentioned a dream of my own. Well, it was nothing. Still it had something about a murder in it. Otherwise I suppose I shouldn't have thought it worth telling.

Tap-tap-tap.   30

If I went in, what, after all, could I do? Fears are intangible things, but they distort the features. It must be curious to see people looking very much frightened. Would their eyes bulge, their fingers twitch, their mouths be twisted into some unmeaning expression? As a general proposition it would be quite amusing. But to see one's sister in that   35
deplorable condition! She would probably be in bed, clutching the

sheet, peering over the edge or perhaps chewing it, the first symptom of
feeble-mindedness! Very likely, though, she would be huddled up
under the bedclothes, a formless lump that I should be tempted to
smack! But there are people who shrink from covering their heads, lest   40
someone should come and hold down the bedclothes and stifle them.
It is not very pleasant to think of such a person bending over you. . . .
Perhaps the child wouldn't be in bed; she would have to get out to
knock. At first I might not see her at all; she might be crouching behind
some piece of furniture, or even hidden in the wardrobe with her head   45
among the hooks. I should have to strike a match. How often they go
out; you throw them on the carpet, and the smouldering head burns a
little hole.
   Tap-tap.
   Minutes passed, and the knocking was not renewed. I turned over.   50
The bed was comfortable enough, but I felt I should sleep sounder if
my sister changed her room. This, after all, could easily be arranged.

1. When the writer woke up he was surprised to find he was
   A refreshed
   B clear-headed
   C afraid
   D bleary-eyed
   E dreaming

2. Which one of the following words is closest in meaning to 'lucidity' as
   used in line 4?
   A Clarity
   B Skill
   C Rationality
   D Success
   E Ability

3. Which one of the following words is closest in meaning to 'odious' as
   used in line 7?
   A Lurking
   B Disease-ridden
   C Repulsive
   D Evil-smelling
   E Annoying

4. According to the first paragraph, when the writer realised he was awake,
   he had already been thinking for some seconds about:
   A the way the blind cord was moving
   B where the bluebottle had gone
   C what had stopped him sleeping
   D what the bluebottle was doing
   E the stillness of the night

5. What answer does the writer arrive at in answer to his question, 'How had I come to wake up?' (lines 4–5)?
   A He had heard someone tapping.
   B The night was still.
   C He had had enough sleep.
   D The blind cord had moved.
   E He had heard a bluebottle.

6. Which *three* of the following best summarise the tone of the writer's sister's voice as she went to bed (line 12)? It was
   1. earnest
   2. demanding
   3. domineering
   4. begging
   5. desperate

   A 1, 2, and 3 only
   B 1, 2, and 4 only
   C 1, 3, and 5 only
   D 2, 3, and 4 only
   E 3, 4, and 5 only

7. The writer 'reflected with uneasy amusement' (line 15) on his sister's parting words for all the following reasons *EXCEPT* that
   A they were a little funny
   B she talked to stay up longer
   C they might have been true
   D she relied on him to help
   E they had kept him awake

8. The writer's sister 'gave an effect of stately deliberation to her departure' (lines 16–17) by
   A having a lot to say
   B talking about being murdered
   C insisting on his attention
   D making everyone feel uneasy
   E gaining an extra few minutes

9. The writer's sister tried to stay up a little longer by using all the following tricks *EXCEPT*
   A talking as much as she could
   B pretending to be suddenly interested in something
   C making the family feel sorry she was leaving
   D becoming serious and important in her manner
   E taking time to kiss everyone goodnight

10. 'As I thought' (line 23) shows that the writer
   A realised his sister was up to her tricks
   B was irritated by the constant tapping on the wall
   C knew the noise would wake up the house
   D could now explain why he had woken up
   E feared his sister was in some kind of danger

11. When the writer heard the 'tap-tap-tap-tap' (line 22) on the wall he
   A knew he would have to do something
   B wondered what was happening next door
   C continued with his line of reasoning
   D decided to call his sister's bluff
   E recognised he had better stay in bed

12. In thinking about 'what had put this silly idea into my sister's head' (line 23) the writer concludes that it most probably came from
   A her own thoughts and imagination
   B something he had once done
   C a story she had invented
   D something a servant had said
   E her own special nightmare

13. Which one of the following is closest in meaning to 'intangible' as used in line 31?
   A Abnormal
   B Unpredictable
   C Terrifying
   D Unexplainable
   E Abstract

14. Which one of the following words best describes the features of someone affected by fear, as the writer imagines them to be in lines 31–35?
   A Paralysed
   B Idiotic
   C Grotesque
   D Sinister
   E Blank

15. Which one of the following could best be used to replace the exclamation mark, without losing its effect, in the sentence, 'But to see one's sister in that deplorable condition!' (lines 35–36)?
   A ... would not be beyond imagining
   B ... would be well worth seeing
   C ... would not be very likely
   D ... would be too horrible for words
   E ... would not be of much help

16. The use of 'feeble-mindedness' (line 38) is a way of avoiding using the blunter word
    A terror
    B foolishness
    C sickness
    D madness
    E depression

17. Which one of the following words is closest in meaning to 'stifle' as used in line 41?
    A Throttle
    B Smother
    C Slaughter
    D Strangle
    E Choke

18. The three dots (. . .) are used in line 42 to suggest that the
    A line of thought is leading nowhere
    B writer cannot find the right words
    C reader can use his own imagination
    D writer is ready to resume the story
    E possibility is not a very likely one

19. The whole of the sixth paragraph (lines 31–48) with its extended reasoning reveals most clearly that the writer
    A enjoys leaving his sister to suffer alone
    B wants to put off going to his sister
    C is already beginning to go back to sleep
    D wants to repay his sister for waking him up
    E has no intention of doing anything at all

20. The fact that the writer does not get up results in a
    A night spent tossing and turning
    B gradual reduction in the tapping
    C decision to go back to sleep
    D growing feeling of deep guilt
    E determination to teach his sister a lesson

Development

Further Reading

1. C. Dickens, *A Christmas Carol*.
   A nightmare with a happy ending.
2. R. A. Banks (ed.), *Ten Ghost Stories*, Hodder and Stoughton, 1978.
   A collection of stories about 'things that go bump in the night'.

Written work

Using most of the details in the story given in the passage, write an account of the evening's events as if you were the little girl herself. (Try to bring out your own feelings and fears as you feel nobody wants to give you any attention.)

Project work

Find out what you can about:
   (*a*) what makes people dream;
   (*b*) three famous dreams and their interpretations and effects. (You might like to include Pharoah's dreams in *Genesis* XLI or Nebuchadnezzar's dream in *Daniel* IV, both of which are given in *The Bible*.)
   (*c*) a book based entirely on a dream:
      e.g. (i) John Bunyan, *The Pilgrim's Progress*, first published in 1678 – the story of man's journey from the City of Destruction through the Slough of Despond, the Valley of the Shadow of Death, Doubting Castle, the Delectable Mountains to the Eternal City.
      (ii) Catherine Storr, *Marianne Dreams*, Faber and Faber, 1958. Marianne is ill in bed, draws a house, and dreams herself into it. The atmosphere is one of fear and its central subject is the hurt that one person can do to another.
      (iii) Philippa Pearce, *Tom's Midnight Garden*, Oxford University Press, 1958.
         Tom is staying in a large house and when the grandfather clock strikes thirteen he finds himself in the large garden back in Victorian times with a Victorian friend, Hatty. On the last day of his stay Tom meets an old lady, Mrs Bartholomew, at the top of the house. She turns out to be Hatty; every night she has been dreaming Tom into her own past life. This is a first-class story of imagination: the atmosphere and sense of mystery are superbly built up.

Exploration 10

Read the following passage very carefully; then answer the questions which follow. *DO NOT GUESS.*

The Rattlesnake

I was in no mood to exchange saucy words. I went and cut myself a long stick and cautiously approached the rattlesnake, in the hope of being able to pin him down and pick him up. However, the reptile had other ideas on the subject. He struck twice at the descending stick and then wriggled towards me rapidly with such obvious menace that I had to   5
perform a ballerina-like leap. The snake by now was in the worst possible temper and, what was more annoying, stubbornly refused to be frightened or cajoled into leaving the research camp site. We tried throwing clods of earth at him, but he just coiled up and rattled. Then I threw a bucket of water over him. This worsened his obviously already   10
high blood-pressure, and he uncoiled and wriggled towards me. The irritating part of the whole business was that we could not just leave him there to make off in his own time. There was work to be done, and one's work is rather apt to suffer by continually having to look over one's shoulder to make sure a four-foot rattlesnake isn't there to be   15
stepped on.
  Very reluctantly, I decided that the only thing to be done was to despatch the infuriated snake as quickly and as painlessly as possible; so, while my wife attracted his attention with the aid of the stick, I approached him cautiously from behind, manoeuvred into position,   20
and sliced off his head with the machete. His jaws kept on snapping for a full minute after his head had been severed from his body, and half an hour later you could still see slight muscular contractions if you touched his ribs with the stick. The extraordinary thing about this snake was that rattlesnakes normally cannot strike unless they are   25
coiled up – so as a rule, however angry one gets, they will always stay coiled up in one position ready to bite – this one, on the other hand, seemed to have had no hesitation in uncoiling and coming straight for you. Whether he could have bitten us successfully with his body stretched out was rather a moot point, but it was not the sort of   30
experiment that I cared to make.

1. The writer 'was in no mood to exchange saucy words' (line oo) because
   A he was becoming more and more angry
   B the snake did not understand language
   C he hated having to deal with snakes
   D the snake had no intention of leaving
   E he felt he was in some danger

2. 'The reptile had other ideas on the subject' (lines 3–4) means that the snake
   A had no intention of being caught
   B was waiting for the stick to fall
   C had decided to move to the attack
   D was making up its mind what to do
   E had no idea what was happening

3. Which two of the following were involved in the snake's action when it 'struck' at the stick (lines 4–6)?
   1. Spitting
   2. Lunging forward
   3. Biting
   4. Coiling up
   5. Stinging

   A 1 and 2 only
   B 1 and 4 only
   C 2 and 3 only
   D 3 and 5 only
   E 4 and 5 only

4. Which one of the following words is closest in meaning to 'menace' as used in line 5?
   A Danger
   B Hostility
   C Threat
   D Venom
   E Rage

5. The comparison of the writer's jump with the leap of a ballerina (line 6) was intended to emphasise which *two* of the following
   1. Its height
   2. Its grace
   3. Its speed
   4. Its lightness
   5. Its skill

   A 1 and 2 only
   B 1 and 3 only
   C 2 and 5 only
   D 3 and 4 only
   E 4 and 5 only

6. After the attack on him with the stick, the rattlesnake was all the following *EXCEPT*

A angry
B unforgiving
C obstinate
D uncowed
E aggressive

7. Which one of the following words is closest in meaning to 'cajoled' as used in line 8?
A Forced
B Coaxed
C Chased
D Compelled
E Persuaded

8. Which *one* of the following was the probable reason why the writer 'threw a bucket of water over him' (lines 9–10)? In order to
A make him docile
B drive him off
C make him uncoil
D cool him down
E make him immobile

9. According to the first paragraph, the writer tried to cajole the snake 'into leaving the camp site' (line 8) because
A its attitude had become very aggressive
B they needed to take over its territory
C they were tired of its nasty temper
D they wanted to get out of the camp
E its presence stopped them from doing any work

10. According to the first paragraph, the writer found the snake's presence all the following *EXCEPT*
A terrifying
B dangerous
C obstructive
D distracting
E annoying

11. Which one of the following words is closest in meaning to 'reluctantly' as used in line 17?
A Gradually
B Unwillingly
C Unavoidably
D Unemotionally
E Deliberately

12. Which one of the following is closest in meaning to 'despatch' as used in line 18?
   A Dispose of
   B Remove
   C Calm down
   D Kill
   E Send away

13. The writer managed to gain a final advantage over the snake wih the help of his wife by
   A tormenting it
   B making it angry
   C distracting it
   D pinning it down
   E prodding it

14. Which one of the following is closest in meaning to 'machete' as used in line 21?
   A Pointed sword
   B Double axe
   C Heavy knife
   D Slender billhook
   E Sharp chopper

15. The snake's 'jaws kept on snapping for a full minute after his head had been severed' (lines 21–22) probably due to
   A reflex actions
   B muscular spasms
   C rigor mortis
   D tense nerves
   E heart tremors

16. Which *three* of the following are the normal actions of a rattlesnake used in attacking a victim?
   1. Biting
   2. Lunging suddenly forward
   3. Spitting
   4. Staying coiled up
   5. Stinging

   A 1, 2, and 3 only
   B 1, 2, and 4 only
   C 1, 3, and 5 only
   D 2, 4, and 5 only
   E 3, 4, and 5 only

17. The rattlesnake described in the passage differed from all others in its
    A way of uncoiling
    B refusal to move
    C hostility to men
    D readiness to fight
    E method of attack

18. Which one of the following words is closest in meaning to 'moot' as used in line 20?
    A Scientific
    B Nice
    C Debatable
    D Good
    E Delicate

19. The last sentence (lines 29–31) suggests that the writer was a man who was particularly
    A cautious
    B unscientific
    C ruthless
    D uninquisitive
    E selfish

20. Which one of the following best summarises the main subject of the passage?
    A A particularly violent rattlesnake attacked a group of research scientists but was immediately outwitted and finally killed with a single machete blow.
    B Rattlesnakes normally strike at their victims from a coiled-up position but a scientist noticed that one representative of the species moved horizontally into attack.
    C A scientist tried to drive a stubborn rattlesnake from his camp site but, after being menaced and attacked, he was compelled reluctantly to kill it.
    D Scientists try to investigate and preserve natural life but on this occasion a hostile and unrepresentative rattlesnake had to be exterminated.
    E A clash between a rattlesnake and a scientist at a camp site was so violent that an experiment under way had to be stopped.

Development

Further reading

1. Rudyard Kipling, *Jungle Books*, 1894–5.
   Read especially the story of the mongoose Rikki-tikki-tavi who defended his adopted family against the attacks of a particularly nasty snake.

2. Gerald Durrell, *The Drunken Forest*, Penguin, 1971.
This is an account of a journey made by Gerald Durrell and his wife to South America.

Written work

1. Animals you have known: write an account of some of the animals you have liked *and* disliked.
2. In 1983 the Chinese sought to reduce their population of dogs by mass extermination. What arguments for and against such a policy for your own country can you find?
3. There have recently been a number of incidents reported where exotic (and sometimes highly dangerous) creatures have been kept as pets: *e.g.* a tarantula or a black widow spider; a crocodile; a panther cub. Imagine that you are such a creature kept as a pet. Give an account of your thoughts and adventures.

Discussion

1. How far should animals be used in scientific experiments intended to benefit mankind?
2. Which *five* living creatures does man need most? Justify your choices.

Project work

Investigate and describe the variety of wild life to be found in the area where you live. (Make use of Natural History books and encyclopaedias to help you with your descriptions.)

A Poem to read and enjoy

(Compare the poet's thoughts and actions with those of the writer of the passage).

Snake

A snake came to my water-trough
On a hot, hot day, and I in pyjamas for the heat,
To drink there.
In the deep, strange-scented shade of the great dark carob-tree
I came down the steps with my pitcher
And must wait, must stand and wait, for there he was at the trough
    before me.

He reached down from a fissure in the earth-wall in the gloom
And trailed his yellow-brown slackness soft-bellied down, over the edge of
    the stone trough
And rested his throat upon the stone bottom.
And where the water had dripped from the tap, in a small clearness,
He sipped with his straight mouth,

Softly drank through his straight gums, into his slack long body,
Silently.

Someone was before me at my water-trough
And I, like a second comer, waiting.

He lifted his head from his drinking, as cattle do,
And looked at me vaguely, as drinking cattle do,
And flickered his two-forked tongue from his lips, and mused a moment,
And stooped and drank a little more,
Being earth-brown, earth-golden from the burning, burning bowels
    of the earth.
On the day of Sicilian July, with Etna smoking.
The voice of my education said to me
He must be killed,
For in Sicily the black, black snakes are innocent, the gold are
    venomous.
And voices in me said, 'If you were a man
You would take a stick and break him now, and finish him off.'

But must I confess how I liked him,
How glad I was he had come like a guest in quiet, to drink at my
    water-trough
And depart peaceful, pacified and thankless,
Into the burning bowels of this earth?

Was it cowardice, that I dared not kill him?
Was it perversity, that I longed to talk to him?
Was it humility, to feel so honoured?
I felt so honoured.

And yet those voices:
If you were not afraid, you would kill him!

And truly I was afraid, I was most afraid,
But even so, honoured still more
That he should seek my hospitality
From out the dark door of the secret earth.
He drank enough
And lifted his head, dreamily, as one who has drunken,
And flickered his tongue like a forked night on the air, so black,
Seeming to lick his lips,
And looked around like a god, unseeing, into the air,
And slowly turned his head,
And slowly, very slowly, as if thrice adream,
Proceeded to draw his slow length curving round
And climb again the broken bank of my wall-face.

And as he put his head into that dreadful hole,

And as he slowly drew up, snake-easing his shoulders, and entered
  farther,
A sort of horror, a sort of protest against his withdrawing into that
  horrid black hole,
Deliberately going into the blackness, and slowly drawing himself after,
Overcame me now his back was turned.

I looked round, I put down my pitcher,
I picked up a clumsy log
And threw it at the water-trough with a clatter.

I think it did not hit him,
But suddenly that part of him that was left behind convulsed in
  undignified haste,
Writhed like lightning, and was gone
Into the black hole, the earth-lipped fissure in the wall-front,
At which, in the intense still noon, I stared with fascination.
And immediately I regretted it.
I thought how paltry, how vulgar, what a mean act!
I despised myself and the voices of my accursed human education.
And I thought of the albatross*,
And I wished he would come back, my snake.
For he seemed to me again like a king,
Like a king in exile, uncrowned in the underworld,
Now due to be crowned again.

And so, I missed my chance with one of the lords
Of life.
And I have something to expiate;
A pettiness.

D. H. Lawrence (1885–1930)

* The albatross, a bird of good omen, was shot by the Ancient Mariner with his cross-bow.
The killing of such a magnificent bird brought nightmare and horror to the ship and its crew.
See *The Ancient Mariner* by S. T. Coleridge (1772–1834).

Exploration 11

Read the following passage carefully; then answer the questions which follow. *DO NOT GUESS*.

Grabbing Your Attention

DO SOME ADVERTISERS GO TOO FAR TO ATTRACT YOUR ATTENTION?

1. Every week hundreds of thousands of advertisements appear for the first time.

Some stand out from the multitude by virtue of their relevance, wit or charm.

Others for less creditable reasons. It is our job as the Advertising Standards Authority to look into any serious malpractices, and make sure that they don't happen again.

2. HOW FAR CAN AN ADVERTISER GO?

This is a vexed question because sometimes there is a very fine line between what is above board and what is below the belt.

One rule in our Code states, 'Advertisements should contain nothing which is likely, in the light of generally prevailing standards of decency and propriety, to cause grave or widespread offence'.

There is no doubt at all what we would do with an ad for a 'video nasty' that depicted someone being eaten alive.

But what about a car advertisement which addressed the reader as 'Ye of little faith'?

A few people might regard it as offensive, but not, we think, the majority.

Although the phrase is of biblical origin, it has slipped into common usage as a metaphor for the sceptical.

3. PREVENTING UNDERHAND TACTICS.

Another rule states. 'Advertisements should not without justifiable reason play on fear'.

What is 'justifiable', and what isn't?

Again we take the view we think the majority would.

We might regard an ad acceptable if it showed how a widow and her children were able to survive on the proceeds of her deceased husband's life assurance.

While offering an answer to a frightening problem it doesn't in itself induce fear.

But suppose a security firm sent a leaflet through the post that said 'I'm a burglar, and I can get into your house as easily as this leaflet'.

This could terrify an older person living alone, and we would do everything within our power to put a stop to it.

4. WHO CAN WE THROW THE BOOK AT?.

The British Code of Advertising Practice covers newspapers, magazines, cinema commercials, posters, brochures, leaflets, circulars posted to you, and now commercials on video tapes.

5. WHY WE ASK YOU TO GRAB A PEN.

Unfortunately some advertisers are unaware of the Code, and breach the rules unwittingly.

Others forget, bend or deliberately ignore the rules. That is why we keep a continuous check on advertising.

But because of the sheer volume we cannot monitor every advertiser all the time.

So we encourage the public to help by telling us about advertisements they think ought not to have appeared.

Last year over 7,500 people wrote to us.

Every complaint is considered and every ruling we make is published in our monthly bulletin.

6. WHAT WE DO TO THE BULLY-BOYS.

If we decide there has been a breach of any rules we ask the advertiser to amend the advertisement. If he cannot, or refuses, we ask him to withdraw it completely.

Nearly all agree without further argument.

In any case we inform the publishers, who will not knowingly accept any ad which we have decided contravenes the Code.

If the advertiser refuses to withdraw the advertisement he will find it hard if not impossible to have it published.

7. CAN ADVERTISERS PUSH US AROUND.

The ASA was not created by law and has no legal powers. Not unnaturally some people are sceptical about its effectiveness.

In fact the ASA was set up by the advertising business to make sure the system of self control genuinely worked in the public interest.

For this to be credible, the ASA has to be totally independent of the business. Neither the chairman nor the majority of ASA council members is allowed to have any involvement in advertising.

Though administrative costs are met by a levy on the business, no advertiser has any influence over ASA decisions.

Advertisers are aware it is as much in their interests as the public's to uphold advertising standards.

If you would like to know more about the ASA and the rules it seeks to enforce you can write to us at the address below for an abridged copy of the Code.

The Advertising ✔
Standards Authority.
If an advertisement is wrong,
we're here to put it right.

ASA Ltd, Dept. A, Brook House,
Torrington Place, London WC1E 7HN.

1. The opening question implies that, in order to attract attention, some
   advertisers
   A break the law
   B spend too much
   C become rather ridiculous
   D overstep the bounds
   E abandon all morality

Section One

2. For which *three* of the following reasons do some advertisements 'stand
   out from the multitude'?
   1. They show many moral qualities.
   2. They keep to the point.
   3. They play cleverly on words.
   4. They have a special attraction.
   5. They try to please everyone.

   A 1, 2, and 3 only
   B 1, 2, and 5 only
   C 1, 3, and 5 only
   D 2, 3, and 4 only
   E 3, 4, and 5 only

3. Which one of the following words is closest in meaning to 'creditable'?
   A Noticeable
   B Deliberate
   C Honourable
   D Convincing
   E Arguable

4. The job of the Advertising Standards Authority is to
   A investigate and stop breaches of their code
   B pursue and prosecute any criminal advertisers
   C examine and regulate products that are advertised
   D censor and change anything they disapprove of
   E advise and ensure their rules are obeyed

Section Two

5. Which one of the following is closest in meaning to 'a vexed question'? A
   question which is
   A important
   B unanswerable
   C troublesome
   D unclear
   E rhetorical

6. 'What is below the belt' is what is
   A confusing
   B unfair
   C disreputable
   D unacceptable
   E hidden

7. The 'one rule in our Code' which is quoted says that advertisements must not
   A challenge any of society's ideas
   B contain references to anything criminal
   C raise questions of any kind
   D become offensive to standards of morality
   E break any of the practices laid down

8. In the light of an earlier remark it is odd to find in the reference to 'a video nasty' the detail that someone might be 'eaten alive' since
   A some might find it offensive
   B it is an unnecessary fact
   C some might laugh at it
   D it distracts the reader's attention
   E some might be influenced by it

9. The reference to 'Ye of little faith', it is suggested, might offend some people because it is
   A a rhetorical question
   B in old-fashioned language
   C a biblical quotation
   D in an incomplete form
   E a metaphorical remark

Section Three

10. The example quoted of the life assurance advertisement is given to show that it is sometimes acceptable to
    A recognise things people fear
    B refer to widows and orphans
    C encourage people to buy assurance
    D explain how to save wisely
    E remind people of death

11. The 'burglar advertisement' from a security firm uses underhand tactics because it might
    A make some vulnerable people afraid
    B encourage burglars to steal
    C make old people stay in
    D claim dishonestly to give protection
    E make burglars' work easier.

Section Four

12. Which one of the following is closest in meaning to 'throw the book at'
    as used in the opening question to this section?
    A Accuse and utterly condemn
    B Keep a close watch on
    C Put finally out of business
    D Bring influence to bear on
    E Force to toe the line

13. Section Four changes the style of presenting the argument by, for the
    first time,
    A making use of examples
    B introducing colloquial language
    C avoiding asking direct questions
    D introducing irrelevant ideas
    E addressing the reader directly

Section Five

14. Which one of the following words is closest in meaning to 'unwittingly'?
    A Reluctantly
    B Unconsciously
    C Carelessly
    D Unreasonably
    E Clumsily

15. The Authority keeps 'a continuous check on advertising' because
    A the Code is abused by some
    B advertisements are always being changed
    C the Code needs revising at times
    D advertisements appear in large numbers
    E the Code is unknown to some

16. Which three of the following provide the biggest headaches for the
    Authority?
        1. Ignorance of advertisers
        2. Poor response to advertisements
        3. Quantity of advertisements
        4. Poor quality of advertisements
        5. Abuse by advertisers

    A 1, 2, and 3 only
    B 1, 2, and 4 only
    C 1, 3, and 5 only
    D 2, 4, and 5 only
    E 3, 4, and 5 only

17. The public are asked to 'grab a pen' because
    A some advertisers ignore the law
    B complaints are taken very seriously
    C some are exploited by advertisers
    D rules need to be changed
    E some advertisements may go unchecked.

Section Six

18. Which *three* of the following are measures the Authority can take against an offensive advertisement?
    1. Ask for it to be changed
    2. Have the advertiser prosecuted
    3. Ask publishers to refuse it
    4. Have the advertiser banned
    5. Ask for it to be withdrawn

    A 1, 2, and 3 only
    B 1, 2, and 4 only
    C 1, 3, and 5 only
    D 2, 4, and 5 only
    E 3, 4, and 5 only

Section Seven

19. Which one of the following words means 'sceptical'?
    A Hesitant
    B Suspicious
    C Doubtful
    D Hostile
    E Apathetic

20. *Section Seven* points to three possible weaknesses about the Advertising Standards Authority, namely, that
    1. it carries no force in law
    2. advertisers support it for wrong reasons
    3. it was established by advertisers
    4. advertisers maintain it by contributions
    5. it has no independent staff

    A 1, 2, and 3 only
    B 1, 2, and 5 only
    C 1, 3, and 4 only
    D 2, 4, and 5 only
    E 3, 4, and 5 only

Development

Written work

1. Write a letter to The Advertising Standards Authority complaining about some aspect of their own 'advertisement'.
2. Devise an advertisement *either* in the form of a radio or TV commercial *or* in the form of a newspaper or magazine feature for the product you most enjoy. (Make sure that you observe the Code!)

Project work

1. Devise a brochure within your group or class to advertise your school or college. (Imagine that recently it has received some adverse publicity and that the purpose of your brochure is to restore its image.)
2. Make a collection of all the advertisements you can find in one edition of a Sunday newspaper's colour supplement; then try to group them under one of the following headings: Product; Reader aimed at; Style.

Further reading

1. G. Dyer, *Advertising as Communication*, Methuen, 1982.
   This book deals with the history, economics, social significance, and analysis of advertising. It is a study book for those interested in advertising.
2. H. Heiber, *Goebbels*, Robert Hale and Co., 1972.
   The most dangerous – and the most interesting – people who try to sell you something are those who try to 'sell' you ideas. One of the most successful sellers of ideas this century was Hitler's Minister of Propaganda, Joseph Goebbels, who committed suicide with his family in the Berlin bunker where his Führer also died in the last days of the 1939–1945 war. This book is an interesting biography.

Exploration 12

Read the following passage carefully; then answer the questions which follow. *DO NOT GUESS.*

St Anthony's Fire

Panic gripped the small French village of Pont-Saint-Esprit in August, 1951. It was as if an immediate collective hysteria of mediaeval intensity had been visited upon the community. Contemporary English language newspapers dealt only briefly with the story, but a full account is given in *The Day of St Anthony's Fire* by John G. Fuller. 5 Hundreds of inhabitants felt the symptoms: giddiness, diarrhoea, vomiting, shaking, and other effects. But for many the experience was much more alarming. Five-year-old Marie-Joseph Carle, for example, saw tigers by the wall and they were coming to eat her. Her father found himself endlessly counting the six panes on his window, day and 10 night; flies were everywhere and he yearned for bead curtains for them to rest on. A young engineer could think of nothing but potatoes. A certain M. Delacquis saw exploding flowers, and knew the secrets of the universe.

It grew worse. Lying in his bedroom, M. Sauvet became a circus 15 performer, a strong man whose pillow cases turned to iron bars which he ripped to shreds effortlessly. Giant timbers splintered in his hands while an invisible audience of admirers cheered deliriously – his bedstead was ruined. One night his night-clothes became leotards. He strutted from his bedroom and into the streets, reaching a temporary 20 suspension bridge over the Rhône, where for fifteen minutes he performed a tightrope act high above the watching villagers. He was rescued, jerking and trembling on a cable, by two gendarmes.

Joseph Puche thought he was an aeroplane. He leapt from a second-storey window shouting, 'I can fly! Don't all of you believe me? 25 Watch!' He shattered both of his legs. Bleeding severely, he rose on two broken legs and ran fifty metres down a boulevard before they caught him; it took eight men and two doctors to get him to hospital.

The hospital itself was overflowing with victims of delusion, shrieking and moaning night after night. One man was being chased by 30 bandits with huge donkey ears. Another was tormented by writhing red snakes in his brain. One woman spat fire from her fingers; another thought she was a baroness and deserved better treatment than she was getting.

There were only three strait-jackets in the hospital, and though the 35 place was ringed by police and firemen, moaning patients were constantly breaking loose and carrying their horrors back into the streets.

And the cause of this appalling visitation? A batch of loaves made by a village baker had been affected by ergot fungus which forms on certain grains and which causes psychic disturbance (LSD is an ergot alkaloid). Ergotism had been thought a thing of the past. In the Middle Ages, whole villages had sometimes been afflicted with a terrifying collective madness which was known as St Anthony's fire; the episode in Pont-Saint-Esprit was a freak recurrence of the ancient malady. Five people died, and of the 300 or so affected by the 'accursed bread' there were many who never truly recovered from their ordeal.

40

45

1. Which one of the following words is closest in meaning to 'panic' as used in line 1?
   A Madness
   B Disaster
   C Alarm
   D Terror
   E Sickness

2. The 'hysteria' (line 2) which came to the village of Pont-Saint-Esprit in 1951 seemed to be all the following *EXCEPT*
   A vigorous
   B sudden
   C common
   D fateful
   E contagious

3. 'Contemporary' (line 3) means
   A of the same period
   B given to sensationalism
   C of a simple kind
   D fond of criticising
   E of the political left

4. The *Day of St. Anthony's Fire* (line 5) is printed in italics because it was a
   A headline
   B TV programme
   C book's title
   D magazine article
   E quotation

5. Which *one* of the following was the most terrifying symptom of the trouble that hit the village?
   A Dizziness
   B Purging
   C Hallucinating
   D Trembling
   E Sickness

6. The experiences of Marie-Joseph Carle, her father, and M. Delacquis described in lines 8–14 included all the following *EXCEPT*
   A fear
   B obsession
   C craving
   D illusion
   E boredom

7. The audience which watched M. Sauvet destroy his bed and bedclothes was 'invisible' (line 18) because it was
   A imaginary
   B delirious
   C hidden
   D ashamed
   E distant

8. 'Leotards' (line 19) are garments which are essentially
   A delicately thin
   B skin-tight
   C brightly coloured
   D makeshift
   E highly restrictive

9. All the following were marked features of Mr. Sauvet's 'tightrope act' (line 22) *EXCEPT* that he
   A thought he was part of a circus
   B was dressed only in his nightclothes
   C managed to keep his balance quite well
   D had an audience far below him
   E lacked any sense of danger whatsoever

10. Which one of the following words is closest in meaning to 'gendarmes' (line 23)?
    A Firemen
    B Soldiers
    C Policemen
    D Rescuers
    E Workmen

11. Suffering from his delusion, Joseph Puche 'leapt from a second-storey window' (lines 24–25) mainly in order to
    A prove his claim
    B terrify his spectators
    C escape his critics
    D outdo his competitors
    E entertain his audience

12. A 'boulevard' (line 27) is a road distinguished because it is which *two* of the following?
    1. Residential
    2. Traffic-free
    3. Wide
    4. Tree-lined
    5. Private

    A 1 and 2 only
    B 1 and 4 only
    C 2 and 5 only
    D 3 and 4 only
    E 4 and 5 only

13. Which two of the following best describe Joseph Puche after he had fallen from the second-storey window (lines 24–28)? He was
    1. delirious
    2. comical
    3. violent
    4. embarrassed
    5. abusive

    A 1 and 2 only
    B 1 and 3 only
    C 2 and 4 only
    D 3 and 5 only
    E 4 and 5 only

14. According to lines 6–34 the delusions to which the villagers fell victims included all the following *EXCEPT* feeling
    A tormented
    B important
    C pursued
    D immortal
    E deformed

15. 'Strait-jackets' (line 35) are used in hospitals mainly to
    A calm seriously ill patients
    B punish mad criminals
    C keep patients in bed
    D cure wild delusions
    E restrain the violently insane

16. The patients are described as 'moaning' (line 36) because they were
    A prevented forcibly from leaving the hospital
    B kept in tight, uncomfortable strait-jackets
    C surrounded by police and firemen
    D ignored when they complained over conditions
    E afflicted by mental and physical agony

17. 'Ergot fungus' (line 39) is a kind of
    A bacteria
    B mould
    C parasite
    D shoot
    E husk

18. According to lines 40–45, for centuries before 1951 the madness caused by ergot fungus had been considered
    A rare
    B extinct
    C fatal
    D inevitable
    E natural

19. Which one of the following words is closest in meaning to 'freak' as used in line 44?
    A Odd
    B Fresh
    C Weird
    D Frightful
    E Rare

20. In giving an account in the passage of the outbreak of St. Anthony's fire, the writer has used all the following *EXCEPT*
    A description
    B illustration
    C narration
    D fiction
    E explanation

Development

Further reading

1. J. G. Fuller, *The Day of St. Anthony's Fire*, Hutchinson, 1969.
2. Tim Healey (ed.), *Strange but True*, Octopus Books Ltd., 1983.
   This is a collection of weird tales, the majority of which are taken from newspaper reports: they include accounts of alligators that live in New York's sewers, the 26-year-old Serb who planned to eat a bus, and the day it rained frogs in the Moroccan Sahara.

Written work

1. Give a detailed account of the strangest event that has happened to you so far.

2. Attempt to justify and/or dismiss a belief in one of the following:
   (*a*) that the earth is flat;
   (*b*) that breaking superstitions leads to trouble;
   (*c*) that many physical illnesses are caused by the mind.

Project work

1. Make a list (with summarised descriptions) of as many unexplained phenomena as you can find. You may, if you wish, suggest some explanations of your own.
2. Make a list of as many different events, facts, or beliefs associated with saints as you can find. You may, if you wish, try to show in detail the link between the saint and what you describe.

Read the following passage very carefully; then answer the questions which follow. *DO NOT GUESS.*

The New Teacher

Duddy absconded, almost at once, from the remand home and took possession of an idle pushbike. He rode it back to Stonehill Street, where he arrived on a Saturday afternoon and met Cribble, a small and exceedingly unintelligent boy in 2C. Cribble was wearing a pair of corduroy jeans that took Duddy's fancy. He proposed a swop: the jeans   5
for the bicycle. Cribble readily agreed. The exchange of trousers took place behind a hoarding. Cribble, delighted, rode home on the bicycle. His father was no brighter than the boy, but it occurred to him after a while that his son's possession of a bicycle could not be innocently explained. When Cribble proved unwilling – perhaps unable – to   10
explain how he came to have it ('Someone gave it me'), Mr Cribble took him round to the police station. 'Well,' he told the Head later, 'That's what the police are for, ain't it?' Within an hour the police had called at Duddy's home, in Minter Mansions, where he was being entertained by his family as an awkward guest.   15
    And so it was, that, on the following Monday morning, a Black Maria drew up outside the Stonehill Street gates. The police appeared in the Head's room and asked if they could have the pleasure of Cribble's company. Certain details had to be cleared up.
    Young Mr. Pitt had arrived among us that very morning, fresh and   20
nervous in his first post. The classics were really his subject, he explained, and it might be that Stonehill Street was not the school for him, in the long run. No, we agreed, for neither Latin nor Greek played a large part in the work of the school. But meanwhile, said Charles Radkins, perhaps he would like to come into the library and be briefed.   25
Charles had been increasingly revolted by the treatment of new teachers at Stonehill Street. They were thrown into action with scarcely a word of encouragement, and usually with no attempt at induction. 'You need,' said Charles, 'some straight talking about the character of the school, something about our rules and regulations in so   30
far as we have any. You know what the Head says to them. "If you're reasonably strict, you'll find the boys will respond. The school has quite a good *tone*." Fancy being flung into 4C without even knowing what the rule is about the school bell. Everyone knows what happens: "Please, Sir, time for the bell. I'll go and ring it." Several volunteers   35
offer their help with the task. The lesson ends in chaos.'
    So Charles and I did what we could, informally, for young Mr Pitt,

with the help of young Mr. Wilkins – who had become old Mr Wilkins, in Stonehill Street terms. Talking to young Mr Pitt hardly helped, though, for he was gentle, completely at a loss in this coarse world. We did not need to be told that his first lessons were failures; the noise from the further end of the hall was demonic. Mr Bonnet flew to the rescue with his usual solution – to leave the door of the offending classroom open, and to open his own across the hall, which left young Mr Pitt in a sort of no-man's land, between a smouldering class under his own nose devising newer and quieter torments and a silently sniggering one not far away.

At break the staffroom was full of the news of Duddy's exploit, and of the arrival of the police. I think it was the maladroit use of the Black Maria that had caused the Head to be loftily cross with the police. No, he had said, they could not see Cribble. He was in school, and the Head was not satisfied that there was any good reason for releasing him from school. The police must seek an interview with him in the presence of his parents outside school hours.

'A little high-handed, surely,' was Brent's comment.

At the height of the fuss, I noticed young Mr Pitt standing near the staffroom door, looking pale and appalled. I went across to him. 'You've perhaps gathered what it's all about?' I asked. 'Duddy – the boy they're talking about – used to be here. An old boy of the school, in fact.'

I think it was the phrase 'old boy' that made Mr. Pitt's pallor even more extreme. He repeated it, in a tone of special horror. 'An Old Boy?'

And suddenly I saw the incident as it must appear to young Mr. Pitt, on his first morning at Stonehill Street. (The first of only three, as it unsurprisingly turned out.) An Old Boy had turned up to revisit his school. Now, Old Boys did that in their best suits, with a kind of shy pride, and came up to masters and shook them by the hand, murmuring about their progress in the world of insurance, banking, accountancy, the teaching of classics, perhaps. But here was an Old Boy who turned up in another boy's trousers – in a Black Maria.

In the circumstances, I thought there was something splendidly inadequate about Mr. Pitt's trembling comment, when at last he managed to find his voice. 'Tell me,' he said, 'does this sort of . . . . . happen often?'

40

45

50

55

60

65

70

75

1. 'Duddy . . . took possession of an idle pushbike' (lines 1–2) means that he

   A bought it
   B claimed it
   C stole it
   D rented it
   E borrowed it

2. The writer implies that Cribble's lack of intelligence was very clearly evident from the fact that he
   A belonged to the class 2C
   B was a pupil at Stonehill Street
   C agreed readily to Duddy's suggestion
   D was the son of Mr Cribble
   E went to school on a Saturday

3. Mr Cribble was obviously 'no brighter than the boy' (line 8) because
   A he could not understand what his son said
   B the swop for the bicycle seemed a fair one
   C he took some time to see the obvious truth
   D the disappearance of the jeans remained unexplained
   E he thought his son was being very obstinate

4. Mr Cribble took his son 'round to the police station' (lines 11–12) presumably in order to
   A make the boy talk more freely
   B report his suspicions about the bicycle
   C explain how the boy had the bicycle
   D have a criminal brought to justice
   E recover the jeans the boy had lost

5. Each of the following expressions is used humorously to avoid a much blunter one *EXCEPT*
   A 'Duddy . . . took possession of an idle pushbike' (lines 1–2)
   B 'his son's possession of a bicycle could not be innocently explained (lines 9–10)
   C 'Mr Cribble took him round to the police station' (lines 11–12)
   D 'he was being entertained by his family as an awkward guest' (lines 14–15)
   E the police . . . asked if they could have the pleasure of Cribble's company (lines 15–19)

6. The teachers agreed with Mr Pitt that Stonehill Street might not be 'the school for him, in the long run' (lines 22–23) because
   A it was known as a very tough city school
   B Mr. Pitt's subjects were not important there
   C it was not a very tolerant school
   D Mr. Pitt was new and would want promotion
   E it was not what he was used to

7. 'Meanwhile' (line 24) carries the meaning of
   A 'during the morning'
   B 'now he was there'
   C 'in the present situation'
   D 'on his first day'
   E 'before he left'

8. Charles Radkins offered to 'brief' the young Mr Pitt (line 25) because he
   A felt new teachers needed help and consideration
   B knew the boys would dislike his attitude
   C felt sorry the curriculum missed out the Classics
   D saw he was disappointed when he arrived
   E felt he would want to leave immediately

9. The word *tone* (line 33) is printed in italics in order to show that it was
   A misused
   B surprising
   C quoted
   D meaningless
   E invented

10. Charles Radkins obviously thought that, compared with knowing about the *tone* of the school, knowing about the school bell rule (line 34) was all the following *EXCEPT* more
    A interesting
    B practical
    C relevant
    D fundamental
    E profitable

11. Mr Wilkins 'had become old Mr Wilkins, in Stonehill Street terms' (lines 38–39) for which *two* of the following reasons?
    1. He had been at the school some time.
    2. He was no longer the junior staff member.
    3. He was now accepted by the boys.
    4. He was no longer as fit as before.
    5. He had lost his former youthful appearance.

    A 1 and 2 only
    B 1 and 3 only
    C 2 and 4 only
    D 3 and 4 only
    E 4 and 5 only

12. 'Talking to young Mr Pitt hardly helped' (line 39) because for Stonehill Street teaching Mr Pitt was too
    A weak
    B well-bred
    C stupid
    D well-spoken
    E refined

13. The young Mr Pitt's early problems in the school were mainly due to his
    A lack of training
    B ignorance of children
    C lack of control
    D ignorance of the rules
    E lack of help

14. Which one of the following words is closest in meaning to 'maladroit' as used in line 49?
    A Foolish
    B Clumsy
    C Obvious
    D Deliberate
    E Threatening

15. The writer thought that the Head had been 'loftily cross with the police' (line 50) because
    A the police were wrong to arrest schoolchildren
    B the Head was worried about police threats
    C the police had shown very little sensitivity
    D the Head disliked collaborating with the police
    E the police were trying to twist the law

16. The Head refused the police permission to see Cribble (lines 51–54) on the grounds that
    A his education was more important than the police inquiries
    B the police had no right to be on school premises
    C his parents had the right to be present during questioning
    D the police had shown no consideration for the school
    E his guilt needed more proof than the police had shown

17. Mr Pitt was 'looking pale and appalled' (line 57) because he had
    A had a bad morning with 4C
    B failed to understand what was happening
    C been overcome by what he had heard
    D realised he would never make a teacher
    E had no contact with the police before

18. The writer 'suddenly saw the incident as it must appear to young Mr Pitt' (line 64) when he realised that it
    A had left him stunned and bemused
    B was completely beyond his experience
    C had come after some disastrous classes
    D was totally against his principles
    E had happened on his very first morning

19. As a result of the Duddy episode the young Mr Pitt was all of the following *EXCEPT*
    A drained of colour
    B almost speechless
    C stricken with terror
    D utterly shocked
    E shaking with disbelief

20. Mr Pitt left Stonehill Street on the third day for all the following reasons *EXCEPT* that
    A he could not maintain discipline easily
    B the tone of the school appalled him
    C he felt out of his element
    D the boys had no intention of working
    E he received no real help from anyone

Development

Further reading

Edward Blishen, *Uncommon Entrance*, Thames and Hudson, 1974; *Roaring Boys*, Thames and Hudson, 1975. (Also available in Panther Books.)

Written work

1. Imagine that you were a member of a class during one of Mr Pitt's first lessons at Stonehill Street. Using the information you find in the extract (and adding other details of your own) write an account of what happened:
   (*a*) as an entry in your own personal diary;
   (*b*) a report for your own teacher who was appalled by the behaviour of your class towards Mr Pitt.
2. Describe your own first day at a new school. (Bring out what pleased you, what frightened you, what surprised you, and what appalled you.)

Further activities

1. Arrange for a local clergyman or social worker to visit your class to describe what he or she sees as the major problems caused by young people in your area and to discuss ways in which these problems are best met.
2. Organise a debate on the motion, 'That this House believes that the police should enforce the law more fairly.'

Exploration 14

Read the following passage very carefully; then answer the questions which follow. *DO NOT GUESS.*

The School Record

One day Mark broke the school swimming record. He and I were fooling around in the pool, near a big bronze plaque marked with events for which the school kept records – 50 yards, 100 yards, 220 yards. Under each was a slot with a marker fitted into it, showing the name of the record-holder, his year, and his time. Under '100 YARDS FREE STYLE' there was 'A. HOPKINS PARKER – 1940 – 53.0 SECONDS'. 5

'You mean that record has been up there *the whole time* we've been at the school and nobody's busted it yet?' It was an insult to the class and Mark had tremendous loyalty to the class. 10

No-one else happened to be in the pool. Around us gleamed white tile and brick; the green, artificial-looking water rocked about in its shining basin, releasing vague chemical smells and a sense of many pipes and filters. Even Mark's voice, trapped in this close, high-ceilinged room, lost its special resonance and mingled into a general 15 wall of noise gathered up towards the ceiling. He said blurringly, 'I have a feeling *I* can swim faster than A. Hopkins Parker.'

We found a stop-watch in the office. He mounted a starting-box, leaned forward from the waist as he had seen racing swimmers do but never had had occasion to do himself – I noticed a preparatory 20 looseness coming into his shoulders and arms, a controlled ease about his stance which was unexpected in anyone trying to break a record. I said, 'On your mark – GO!' There was a complex moment when his body uncoiled and shot forward with a metallic tension. He planed up the pool, his shoulders dominating the water, while his legs and feet 25 rode so low that I couldn't distinguish them; a wake rippled hurriedly by him and then at the end of the pool his position broke, he relaxed, dived, an instant's confusion and then his suddenly and metallically tensed body shot back towards the other end of the pool. Another turn and up the pool again – I noticed no slackening of his pace – another 30 turn, down the pool again, his hand touched the end, and he looked up at me with a composed, interested expression. 'Well, how did I do?' I looked at the watch; he had broken A. Hopkins Parker's record by seven-tenths of a second.

'So I really did it! You know what? I thought I was going to do it. It 35 felt as though I had that stop watch in my head and I could hear myself going just a little bit faster than A. Hopkins Parker.'

'The worst thing is there weren't any witnesses. And I'm no official time-keeper. I don't think it will count.'

'Well, of course it won't *count*.' 40

'You can try it again and break it again. Tomorrow.'

He climbed out of the pool. 'I'm not going to do it again,' he said quietly.

'Of course you are!'

'No, I just wanted to see if I could do it. Now I know. But I don't 45 want to do it in public. By the way,' he said in an even more subdued voice, 'we aren't going to talk about this. It's just between you and me.'

Was he trying to impress me or something? Not tell anybody? When he had broken the school record without a day of practice? The record board now contained a mistake, a lie, and nobody knew it but Mark and 50 me.

'Swimming in pools is screwy, anyway,' he said after a long, unusual silence as we walked away. 'The only real swimming is in the ocean.' I knew he was serious about it, so I didn't tell anybody.

1. Which one of the following colloquial expressions is closest in meaning to 'fooling around' as used in line 2?
   A Loafing around
   B Splashing around
   C Messing around
   D Gadding around
   E Fiddling around

2. Which one of the following words is closest in meaning to 'plaque' as used in line 2?
   A Tablet
   B Board
   C Notice
   D List
   E Chart

3. The words *the whole time* (line 8) are in italics to show that they
   A were somewhat unusual
   B have been used ungrammatically
   C were directly quoted
   D have been specially included
   E were particularly stressed

4. The reason why Mark was so outraged that the record had not been 'busted' (line 9) was that it had
   A been ignored by his whole class
   B escaped his attention all the time
   C been one so easy to beat
   D posed a threat to the class's honour
   E been prominent enough on the bronze plaque

5. Mark spoke 'blurringly' (line 16) because
   A he was very excited
   B the ceiling was high
   C he was naturally embarrassed
   D the water absorbed noise
   E he was thinking aloud

6. According to the third paragraph (lines 11–17), the room with the pool
   was all the following *EXCEPT*
   A almost deserted
   B shining bright
   C somewhat antiseptic
   D rather high
   E strangely silent

7. Which *one* of the following must have happened for certain between the
   circumstances set out in lines 8 and 16?
   A The writer put difficulties in Mark's way.
   B Mark decided to attempt a new record.
   C The writer challenged Mark to a race.
   D Mark went off to get his costume on.
   E The writer left Mark to think things over.

8. All the following were fortunate circumstances for Mark's swim
   EXCEPT the
   A emptiness of the swimming-pool
   B presence of his friend
   C existence of a starting-box
   D stillness of the water
   E discovery of a stop-watch

9. The writer obviously expected anyone about to try 'to break a record'
   (line 22) in swimming to
   A stand straight
   B be relaxed
   C concentrate hard
   D be tense
   E stretch forward

10. The way Mark left the starting-box (lines 23–24) is compared with a
    A spring unwinding suddenly
    B bullet leaving a gun
    C sword thrusting forward
    D trap snapping rapidly open
    E snake uncurling quickly

11. The length of the swimming-pool must have been
    A 25 yards
    B $33\frac{1}{2}$ yards
    C 50 yards
    D $66\frac{2}{3}$ yards
    E 75 yards

12. The way Mark swam to break the record clearly featured all the
    following *EXCEPT*
    A skilful turning
    B strong leg-action
    C consistent speed
    D powerful arm-movement
    E strong finishing

13. The way Mark asked the question 'Well, how did I do?' (line 32)
    suggests that he was
    A much too over-confident
    B secretly fearing the worst
    C scarcely out-of-breath
    D slowly realising the truth
    E far too off-hand

14. Mark's response to the news that he had broken the record (lines 33–34)
    mainly shows his
    A self-consciousness
    B self-confidence
    C self-conceitedness
    D self-concern
    E self-contempt

15. Mark emphasised that the record would not *count* (line 40) because it
    had been made
    A privately
    B inaccurately
    C unexpectedly
    D illegally
    E individually

16. Mark insisted that he was 'not going to do it again' (line 42) because
    he
    A knew he would fail next time in public
    B had done it only for his personal self-satisfaction
    C could hardly believe he had managed it once
    D had little interest in the school's record-breakers
    E felt he must behave modestly with his friends

17. Which one of the following words is closest in meaning to 'subdued' as used in line 46?
    A Toned-down
    B Repressed
    C Off-hand
    D Threatening
    E Screwed-up

18. The writer's initial reaction to Mark's insistence that his record-breaking attempt should remain a secret (line 47) is best described as one of
    A deep distress
    B serious concern
    C utter disbelief
    D extreme irritation
    E total disappointment

19. The writer's accusation that the board 'now contained a mistake, a lie' (lines 49–51) is essentially ill-founded because
    A Mark wanted the secret kept tight
    B the truth was known by two people
    C Mark's record was not officially set
    D the record could easily be corrected
    E Mark's swim had been inaccurately timed

20. The writer's attitude to Mark was most clearly one based on
    A envy
    B respect
    C suspicion
    D rivalry
    E affection

Development

Further activities

1. Consult a record book such as *The Guinness Book of Records* and make a selection of *five* records in each of the following categories:
   (a) those which have demanded, in your view, the greatest courage;
   (b) those which have demanded, in your view, the greatest physical stamina;
   (c) those which have demanded, in your view, the greatest intellectual ability;
   (d) those which seem to you to have been most pointless.

2. Say in about twenty or thirty words which record you would most like to break. **Then** write a reasoned account of why you would like to break the record and what steps you would have to take in order to do so.

Further reading

1. Here are some books which give accounts of the ways some well-known records were broken:
   (*a*) R. Bannister, *The First Four Minutes*, Putnam and Co., 1958.
   (*b*) C. Bonnington, *Everest The Hard Way*, Hodder and Stoughton, 1976.
   (*c*) E. Hillary, *Nothing Venture, Nothing Win*, Hodder and Stoughton, 1975.
2. Some lighter reading:
   (*a*) Stephen Winkworth, *Famous Sporting Fiascos*, Sphere, 1983.
   (*b*) J. L. Foster, *Record Breakers*, Edward Arnold, 1977.
   (*c*) P. Cleaver, *Book of Record Breakers*, Sparrow Books, 1981.
   (*d*) *The Guinness Book of Records*, ed. N. D. McWhirter, 1984.

Read the following passage very carefully; then answer the questions which
follow. *DO NOT GUESS.*

Running Away

He would go very early, even before they did; he would go at dawn.
They would never think of looking into his room. Then, with the house
empty, there would be the whole day, until very late in the evening,
before anyone could possibly find out.

But when his mother got back from London, she would come up and   5
look into his room. He would have to risk it, that was all, or else do
something to the bedclothes. No, that wouldn't work. She always
wanted to lean over him and put her face onto his; she would find out
immediately she came into the room.

He had plenty of money. People gave him pound and ten-shilling   10
notes for Christmas and birthdays. They gave him more because he
hadn't got a father. He never spent much and had almost seven
pounds. If he walked to Crelford station by the road, someone would
be bound to see him. He was going across the country, beginning with
Hang Wood. He had to make himself go into Hang Wood, whether he   15
dared or not. And he could hide and they would never think of looking
there, first.

He had set the alarm for half-past five, and then, after some more
thought, moved it forward to five o'clock. It would be light by then and
he wanted to go as early as he could. He had brought all the things he   20
was taking along from the other room, very late the previous evening
while they had been watching television. Now, they were under his
bed.

The food had been most difficult to get. He had taken it from the
kitchen at the last moment while his mother was out. She would   25
certainly miss it. He wondered whether that was stealing. At school
they said that stealing was one of the worst things you could ever do. In
the end, he had decided that it was not stealing; the food he was taking
was the food he would have eaten if he had not been going away. He
wasn't taking very much in any case, just biscuits, some crisps, and half   30
a box of processed cheeses. He had bought chocolate in the village. It
looked enough and he had money to buy more.

Water was more difficult. A glass bottle would be heavy and might
break, and, in any case, he couldn't find one that was empty. In the end,
he decided to drink a lot before setting out, and then find a stream, or a   35

shop selling lemonade. He had never been into the country before, but
he thought there would be streams.

Besides the food, he packed a torch, his penknife, some sticking
plaster, a pair of socks, and a ball of string. He had not been able to find
a map. There was nothing else he could think of.   40

He woke soon after four o'clock. It was still dark. There was no point
in going yet. He lay stiffly on his back, eyes open. He knew he ought to
care about his mother. He ought to care what she would feel; he had a
sense of there being something wrong with him, because he did not
care. She had brought him here and now she was going to London with   45
Mr Hooper.

He lay until the darkness of the room thinned perceptibly to grey. It
was twenty minutes to five. He would not go yet; he dared not go in the
dark. But he could not lie still. He got up and dressed and stood beside
the window, forcing himself to count his breaths up to ten, in and out,   50
waiting for the alarm to ring.

1. 'They' (line 1) refers to
   A the boy's mother and father
   B the people keeping the boy locked-up
   C those responsible for the boy's trouble
   D the rest of the boy's household
   E the boy's brothers and sisters.

2. The reason why the boy decided to 'go at dawn' (line 1) was that
   then
   A he could have all day before he was missed
   B his absence would not draw attention to itself
   C he would be the first to leave the house
   D his parents did not care much about him
   E he could avoid being seen in the half-light

3. He considered doing 'something to the bedclothes' (line 7) in order to
   A distract his mother from his obvious absence
   B tidy his room up before he left
   C make everyone puzzled about what had happened
   D leave his mother to make his bed
   E make it seem he was already in bed

4. He realised his plan 'wouldn't work' (line 7) because his
   A room always looked in a mess
   B mother always came back early
   C room always attracted his mother
   D mother always came to kiss him
   E room always gave him away

5. The first two paragraphs (lines 1–9) suggest most strongly that
   A the boy preferred doing things to thinking
   B running away always results in failure
   C the boy cared little about other people
   D running away is impossible to plan
   E the boy felt distant from his family

6. For which *two* of the following reasons did the boy have 'plenty of money' (line 10)?
   1. People took pity on him.
   2. He was given expensive presents.
   3. Christmas and birthdays had just occurred.
   4. He had been saving up.
   5. People were always too generous.

   A 1 and 2 only
   B 1 and 4 only
   C 2 and 3 only
   D 3 and 5 only
   E 4 and 5 only

7. According to lines 1–17, the boy's plans for running away involved all the following *EXCEPT*
   A leaving very early
   B laying false trails
   C avoiding main roads
   D hiding in woods
   E avoiding immediate discovery

8. In the boy's plans to escape detection (lines 1–17), he thought all the following might give him away *EXCEPT*
   A his mother's coming into his room on her return
   B the chance of being spotted on the open road
   C arranging his bedclothes in a certain way before leaving
   D going to the station immediately instead of hiding
   E spending too long in the woods before moving on

9. The thought that led the boy to advance the alarm to five o'clock (line 19) was the desire to
   A go as soon as he woke up
   B avoid waking up the whole house
   C depart before the others left
   D avoid missing his chances by oversleeping
   E leave as soon as it was light

10. Judging from lines 1–23, the boy seemed all the following *EXCEPT*
    A lonely
    B resourceful
    C affectionate
    D economical
    E nervous

11. All the following are probable reasons why 'the food had been the most difficult to get' (line 24) *EXCEPT* that
    A it was in the kitchen
    B his mother was usually about
    C it would not keep indefinitely
    D his mother would notice its disappearance
    E it could not be hidden easily

12. Which one of the following thoughts affected the boy's conscience later?
    A He had certainly stolen the food.
    B Stealing was a very bad act.
    C He had never stolen anything before.
    D Stealing was certain to be found out.
    E He had no need to steal food.

13. Which *two* of the following thoughts helped to ease his conscience later?
    1. The food would not be missed.
    2. He had taken very little.
    3. It was food intended for him.
    4. He had bought his own chocolate.
    5. The food had not been expensive.

    A 1 and 2 only
    B 1 and 4 only
    C 2 and 3 only
    D 3 and 5 only
    E 4 and 5 only

14. For which *three* of the following reasons did the boy find 'Water was more difficult' (line 33)?
    1. He could not find a suitable bottle.
    2. It could not be carried very conveniently.
    3. He could not risk going to the kitchen.
    4. It could not be carried with any safety.
    5. He could not hide it very easily.

    A 1, 2, and 3 only
    B 1, 2, and 4 only
    C 2, 3, and 5 only
    D 2, 4, and 5 only
    E 3, 4, and 5 only

15. From evidence found elsewhere in the passage, it is probable, that when he woke soon after four o'clock, the boy saw 'no point in going yet' (lines 41–42) because
    A he was worried about his future
    B the rest of the household was asleep
    C he was uncertain what to do next
    D the equipment he needed was already packed
    E he was afraid of the dark

16. The boy thought he lacked natural affection for his mother (lines 44–45) really because he was
    A resentful
    B spoilt
    C guilt-ridden
    D selfish
    E spiteful

17. Which one of the following words is closest in meaning to 'perceptibly' as used in line 47?
    A Gradually
    B Noticeably
    C Delicately
    D Inevitably
    E Reassuringly

18. Everything the boy did, according to the last paragraph (lines 47–51), suggests that he was all the following *EXCEPT*
    A timid
    B uncertain
    C restless
    D unhappy
    E dazed

19. The underlying reason why the boy wanted to leave home was most probably the
    A wish to make his own way in the world
    B determination to make others suffer as he had suffered
    C feeling that his mother no longer loved him
    D need to embark on a new and dangerous adventure
    E dislike he had of his house and everyone in it

20. All the following show that the boy felt lonely and rejected *EXCEPT*
    A 'They would never think of looking into his room.' (line 2)
    B 'He hadn't got a father.' (lines 11–12)
    C 'He had never been into the country before.' (line 36)
    D 'He knew he ought to care about his mother.' (lines 42–43)
    E 'She was going to London with Mr Hooper.' (lines 45–46)

Development

Further reading

1. Charles Dickens, *Great Expectations*, chapters 1–6.
   This gives an account of a frightening experience suffered by an orphan boy who had gone to live with his sister and her husband; graveyards, an escaped criminal, the stealing of food, and a threat to tear out the boy's heart and liver which will then be roasted are just a few of the more noticeable features of this part of the story.
2. John Collier, *Thus I refute Beelzy*, in R. A. Banks (ed.), *Ten Ghost Stories*, Hodder and Stoughton. 1978.
   In this short story of the supernatural, Small Simon, a strangely withdrawn boy with an over-indulgent mother and a hard father, brings a monster from his world of fantasies into the real world to punish the adults in his house. The last sentence of the story is:

   > It was on the second-floor landing that they found the shoe, with the man's foot still in it, like that last morsel of a mouse which sometimes falls from the jaws of a hasty cat.

Written work

1. Write a series of entries for your own secret, personal diary which tell of your thoughts and feelings at a time in your life when you felt particularly lonely.
2. Find out what you can about the life and work of Dr Thomas Barnardo (1845–1905) who devoted his life to helping destitute children in London's East End.
   Then write an accout of your findings in the form of an entry in a school history *or* sociology text book.
3. Continue the story given in the passage. Try to keep the same style so far as possible but make sure you finish the episode. (You will have to decide what you think happened: Did the boy leave? Did he change his mind? Was he discovered?)

Further activities

1. Find out what you can about *one* organisation whose special work is to help children in need: *e.g.* The National Society for the Prevention of Cruelty to Children (NSPCC); Save the Children Fund; UNICEF; The Spastics Society.
   (Telephone directories and 'Yellow Pages' will give you the addresses of such organisations.)
2. Arrange to see the film *The Sound of Music* and then discuss within your class or group how far this presentation of the happy relationship between a kind, caring adult and a group of deprived children could ever be real.
3. Discuss *either* the problems of living as an 'only child' *or* the difficulties of being a step-child or step-brother/sister.

Exploration 16

Read the following passage very carefully; then answer the questions which follow. *DO NOT GUESS.*

The Motor-Bike*

Some fathers have remarkable double standards about motor cycles. They may recall their own bold exploits down the old A1, when 'a ton-up' really did feel like 100 miles per hour, and yet refuse point blank to allow their sons or daughters to follow suit.

Things are different now, the sages declare. Accidents among motor 5
cyclists are too common. Roads are crowded with careless drivers and a motor cycle is too vulnerable for modern traffic conditions. Certainly the accident statistics are depressingly high, particularly among young drivers, and legislation seems continually to scramble behind the necessity of not allowing learner drivers on the road alone with only a 10
bare minimum of instruction on motor cycles that are lethally fast.

Recently I met a neurologist working at a large northern hospital who remains a convinced motor cyclist in spite of his work. He travels to work every day on a powerful four-cylinder machine and spends much of his time repairing the results of motor cycle accidents. He 15
thought the death rate was relatively lower now than when motor cycles last enjoyed wide popularity. The legal requirement to wear a crash helmet had meant that more riders survived accidents that would otherwise have killed them. His experience convinced him that once through the dare-devil stage, a motor cyclist stood no higher chance of 20
being killed than a car driver.

'What he loses on being vulnerable he gains by being more manoeuvrable on the road. If he is driving properly he can often avoid a crash because he takes up less room and is more agile,' he said.

He also pointed out that modern machines are generally better 25
balanced, with superior steering and braking, than the dreadnoughts father used to ride.

Recently I have returned to two wheels after years of being cocooned between four. My motor cycle is of impeccable pedigree, but languished for years beneath a blanket in a shed. It is a Velocette 30
Venom, one of the famous models produced when Britain ruled the industry and those slick, purring, push-button Japanese machines were barely dreams in the minds of their designers. Its single cylinder carries more tubing and valves than a trumpet and the elegant fishtail exhaust, a distinguishing mark of the model, strangles some of its 35
mettlesome roar.

* © Times Newspapers Ltd, London.

Browsing through a magazine called *Classic Bike*, I discovered my
Venom might be worth more than £1000, some twenty times what I
paid for it. The apprentice who took my Venom for an MoT trial
returned ashenfaced. 'You cannot pass that,' wailed the pampered   40
youth. 'Of course we can; it's a Venom,' rapped out the chief engineer,
who understood these things.

On a late summer day with a dry road the machine was a sheer joy. I
had forgotten the surge of a bike on a snaking road, the tenor warble of
a Venom at speed, the rush of air tearing tears from the eyes and the   45
evocative whiffs of fresh-cut grass, woodsmoke, or road tar that tickle
the nose buds of some motor cyclists. But not all, for the modern 'biker'
misses those sensations because he is likely to have his head encased in
a dome-shaped skull-saver with a visor of transparent plastic hiding his
face. One 'biker' I have met cruises down the M8 at fearsome speed   50
with 'The Ride of the Valkyrie' booming around his helmet. Suits
impenetrable to rain or cold are available with electric heating. They
even help the rider to bounce if he falls off. The modern 'biker' may
look like The Black Knight in search of a joust, but he is better
protected, and in modern traffic needs to be.   55

Motor cycle marketing seems aimed at suggesting that riding a bike
is tough and manly. A shiny machine, bristling with power and exhaust
pipes is somehow an indication of personal potency. It is not that bonus
that has driven me back to my Venom. The 65 miles to the gallon is
appreciated; crossing the Forth Bridge free of tolls and parking in   60
Edinburgh without difficulty and for nothing are worthwhile.

Secretly most satisfying are the vibrations of outrage and envy from
long lines of car-bound fathers as the Venom thumps carefully to the
head of the queue and, with a roar rising to a crescendo, shakes itself
free down the open road.   65

1. Which one of the following is closest in meaning to 'have . . . double
   standards' as used in line 1? To
   A believe that what is sauce for the goose is sauce for the gander
   B have one law for the rich and another for the poor
   C take the law into one's own hands whenever it is convenient
   D have different attitudes to what is essentially the same thing
   E say one thing at one time and something quite different at another

2. Which one of the following is closest in meaning to 'follow suit' as used
   in line 4?
   A Run the same sort of risk
   B Dice it out similarly with death
   C Challenge the same set of rules
   D Dress in exactly the same way
   E Play the same kind of card

3. Which one of the following is closest in meaning to 'sages' as used in line 5?
   A Know-alls
   B Statisticians
   C Wise men
   D Philosophers
   E Smart-Alicks

4. Which one of the following is closest in meaning to 'vulnerable' as used in line 7?
   A Difficult to manage
   B Powerful in performance
   C Open to accidents
   D Modern in design
   E Easy to own

5. 'Things are different now' (line 5) for all the following reasons *EXCEPT* that now
   A motor-cycle accidents have increased
   B laws become quickly out-of-date
   C road conditions are very dangerous
   D machines have dangerously high speeds
   E driving standards are too low

6. A neurologist (line 12) is a doctor who specialises in treating injuries to
   A the limbs
   B the heart and lungs
   C the nervous system
   D the neck and shoulders
   E the muscles

7. The neurologist 'thought the death rate was relatively lower now' (line 16) because
   A learners received better instruction
   B bikes were better made
   C doctors operated more successfully
   D helmets had to be worn
   E cars were driven more carefully

8. 'The dare-devil stage' (line 20) is one marked by all the following *EXCEPT*
   A recklessness
   B danger
   C defiance
   D disaster
   E adventurousness

9. The neurologist believed that the motor-cyclist could offset his or her vulnerability on the road by agility, manoeuvrability, and the fact that
   A braking had vastly improved
   B little road space was needed
   C cars were also at risk
   D increased speed left danger behind
   E balance was much better

10. Which one of the following words is closest in meaning to 'dread-noughts' as used in line 26?
    A Bangers
    B Tanks
    C Death-traps
    D Contraptions
    E Battleships

11. The word 'cocooned' (line 28) used by the writer to describe the way he felt 'closed in' is taken from the study of
    A animals
    B engineering
    C bacteria
    D motoring
    E insects

12. Which one of the following words is closest in meaning to 'impeccable' as used in line 29?
    A Excellent
    B Matchless
    C Traceable
    D Faultless
    E Established

13. The Velocette Venom was a motor cycle characterised by which *two* of the following, in addition to the special 'distinguishing mark of the model'?
    1. Its elaborate pipework
    2. A push-start
    3. The fish-like appearance
    4. A large engine
    5. Its muted exhaust

    A 1 and 2 only
    B 1 and 5 only
    C 2 and 4 only
    D 3 and 4 only
    E 3 and 5 only

14. The apprentice who took the 'Venom for an MoT trial returned ashenfaced' (lines 39–40) because he
    A had had an accident
    B could not drive it
    C knew nothing about it
    D could not pass it
    E had had a shock

15. The youth had been 'pampered' (line 40) because he was familiar with motor cycles which were all the following *EXCEPT*
    A well-maintained
    B slick
    C foreign-made
    D quiet
    E push-button

16. The 'sheer-joy' (line 43) of riding a Venom on a late summer day along a dry road included all the following *EXCEPT* the
    A noise of the engine
    B power of the machine
    C winding of the road
    D shaking of the machine
    E smell of the countryside

17. 'Bikers' with modern equipment can have all the following advantages *EXCEPT* that of
    A avoiding serious injury
    B staying quite warm
    C enjoying broadcast entertainment
    D staying quite dry
    E having protective clothing

18. Which *three* of the following are the reasons why the writer has been driven 'back to my Venom' (line 59)?
    1. Envious looks
    2. Tricks of advertisers
    3. Low running costs
    4. Lust for power
    5. Easy parking

    A 1, 2, and 3 only
    B 1, 2, and 4 only
    C 1, 3, and 5 only
    D 2, 4, and 5 only
    E 3, 4, and 5 only

19. Which one of the following words refers to the shuddering of the motor cycle caused by the engine?
    A 'Vibrations' (line 62)
    B 'Thumps' (line 63)
    C 'Roar' (line 64)
    D 'Crescendo' (line 64)
    E 'Shakes' (line 64)

20. The writer has written this article from the point of view of
    A a mechanic
    B an enthusiast
    C a learner-driver
    D an advertiser
    E a parent

Development

Written work

1. Write an article for a newspaper in response to the passage. In your article point out the dangers and discomfort of motor-cycling in an attempt to persuade the young not to buy the new powerful machines.
2. Set out, in the form of a letter written to your local newspaper, the measures you would take to reduce road accidents.
3. Design an advertisement to increase the sales of motor cycles (or cycles, if you prefer). Decide, before you begin, the age-range and income-bracket of the people at whom you direct your advertisement.
4. Design a 'small-ad' for inclusion in a specialist magazine to sell a motor cycle or a cycle.

Further activities

Arrange for a policeman from the local police station to visit your class to discuss some of the problems caused by motor cycles (or cycles) in your area and ways in which both motor cyclists and cyclists can ride more safely on the roads.

Further reading

1. *The Encyclopaedia of Motor-cycling*, Hamlyn Publishing Group, 1980.
2. F. Alderson, *Bicycling: a History*, David and Charles, 1972.

Exploration 17

Read the following passage very carefully, then answer the questions which follow. *DO NOT GUESS.*

UFOs

In March 1957, villagers at Wardle near Rochdale saw a sinister, glowing object hovering ominously over their small community. From it emanated an eerie white light. So great was the local concern about the UFO that questions were even asked in Parliament about it. Were the aliens poised for invasion? 5

The answer came in the House of Commons, when the Air Minister was questioned about the Rochdale Thing. Amid laughter, an under-secretary replied: 'This object, which was described in the Press as a flying saucer, did not emanate from outer space, but from a laundry in Rochdale. It consisted of two hydrogen-filled balloons illuminated by a 10 torch bulb and devised by a laundry mechanic.'

Questioned by reporters, the mechanic revealed himself to be an amateur meteorologist who had created the device as an experiment in tracing air currents.

The case is just one among many UFO 'flaps'. On New Year's Eve in 15 1978 for example, television viewers throughout Europe were riveted by the screening of some mysterious objects filmed over New Zealand. At the same time, a cigar-shaped craft with flaming portholes was widely reported in Europe itself. A Cheshire surgeon and his neighbour, a builder, were among the first to spot the object. 'It was 20 cigar-shaped with a broad, trailing vapour jet,' said the surgeon. 'It moved in a straight line with no noise. I have always been sceptical about these things, but this defied any orthodox analysis.' His neighbour confirmed the description: he saw 'portholes aflame with incandescence'. 25

Though some controversy still lingers around the New Zealand sightings, the cigar-shaped craft proved easier to explain. It was the burning debris of a Soviet rocket, which had launched the satellite Cosmos 1068 into space and crashed in West Germany.

Unquestionably the most famous flap, however, occurred in the New 30 York area in late October 1938 – before the term 'flying saucer' had even been coined. *The Times* reported: 'All began after 8 o'clock last night, when a dramatisation of Mr H. G. Wells's fantasy *The War of the Worlds* came on the air over the national network of the Columbia broad-casting system. The production was the work of Mr Orson Welles, a young 35 American who is known as an innovator on the New York stage. He dramatizes a book or play every Sunday night on the wireless.'

In Orson Welles's ingenious production, the story was presented in a contemporary American setting. A weather report was given in a deadpan voice, followed by a programme of dance music from a 40
fictional hotel. In the middle of a number, a newsflash was delivered concerning a gas explosion on Mars. Further news bulletins and descriptions followed: A meteor had landed near Princeton, New Jersey, killing 1,500 people. No, it wasn't a meteor, it was a metal cylinder. The top unscrewed – monsters crawled out armed with death 45
rays – bullets could not stop them – they were marching on New York – martial law had been declared and the state militia were out.

The Martians were coming! At least they were as far as hundreds of panic-stricken listeners were concerned. Telephone lines to the police stations were soon jammed. People rushed into the streets, many of 50
them with towels over their faces as gas masks. Less excitable souls telephoned the authorities offering to help in the emergency. Even church services were interrupted.

Three times during the programme it was explained that the events were only part of a radio programme, but these announcements failed 55
to stop the panic. Eventually, a series of reassuring pronouncements from Columbia officials, police and detailed news services did manage to restore peace. Columbia, however, faced heavy criticism in the ensuing days – though the publicity did Orson Welles's career no harm. 60

1. Which one of the following is closest in meaning to 'ominously' as used in line 2?
   A Inauspiciously
   B Threateningly
   C Dangerously
   D Malevolently
   E Inexorably

2. Which one of the following terms is represented by the letters *UFO* (line 4)?
   A Unexplainable Flight Observation
   B Universal Fiery Omen
   C Unexpected Foreign Offensive
   D Universal Forward Operation
   E Unidentified Flying Object

3. All the following were characteristics of the object 'hovering ominously' described in the first paragraph (lines 1–15) *EXCEPT* that it
   A looked very menacing
   B contained alien visitors
   C lingered above the village
   D caused much worry locally
   E shone with heat

4. 'The Rochdale Thing' (line 7) was called a 'Thing' because it
   A became a huge joke
   B had not stayed long
   C seemed a sinister object
   D had not been identified
   E was somebody's own wild invention

5. The House of Commons laughed when an under-secretary described the UFO (lines 7–11) because
   A the members always enjoyed a laugh
   B a practical joke had been played
   C the explanation was wildly improbable
   D a danger had suddenly evaporated
   E the press had acted ridiculously

6. The laundry mechanic (line 11) was also very interested in
   A studying the weather
   B inventing washing machines
   C investigating outer space
   D causing practical jokes
   E meeting the press

7. The word 'flaps' (line 15) is in inverted commas because it is
   A a direct quotation
   B slang
   C a technical term
   D speech
   E an American word

8. The 'mysterious objects filmed over New Zealand' (line 17) is given as an example of
   A a TV programme
   B a phenomenon
   C a practical joke
   D a flap
   E a distant UFO

9. All the following are true of the object seen by the Cheshire surgeon (line 19) *EXCEPT* that it
   A could be explained perfectly logically
   B was seen by two people only
   C seemed to be on fire
   D followed a very definite course
   E came down on the earth's surface

10. 'Orthodox' (line 23) means
    A psychological
    B certain
    C rational
    D simple
    E conventional

11. 'Controversy' (line 26) means
    A doubt
    B concern
    C argument
    D excitement
    E difficulty

12. 'A dramatisation of Mr H. G. Wells's *The War of the Worlds*' (line 33) in 1938 took the form of a
    A book review
    B television programme
    C feature film
    D radio programme
    E theatrical production

13. 'An innovator' (line 00) is someone who
    A produces original plays
    B makes scientific discoveries
    C brings in new ideas
    D sees into the future
    E revises old productions

14. An important feature of Orson Welles's production of H. G. Wells's fantasy that led to the 'flap' was that in America it
    A used all the modern stage devices
    B was placed in a present-day context
    C formed part of a regular broadcast series
    D was immediately recognised as science fiction
    E broke all the normal dramatic rules

15. 'A deadpan voice' (lines 39–40) is one which is
    A unexpected
    B dramatic
    C bored
    D routine
    E emotionless

16. Which *one* of the following in the sequence of dramatic incidents which made up the broadcast of Orson Welles's production is inaccurate in its detail?

A There was an explosion on Mars.
B An object, thought to be a meteor, landed.
C New York was under immediate threat.
D Alien creatures killed 1500 with death rays.
E Military forces had been brought into action.

17. The sentence, 'At least . . . . were concerned' (lines 48–49) is introduced to remind the reader that
A the invaders came from the planet Mars
B fiction is often stranger than fact
C the broadcast was only a dramatisation
D aliens can cause panic among people
E the listeners were rather ignorant people

18. All the following were signs that Orson Welles's programme had been taken literally *EXCEPT* that
A the police were flooded with calls from the public
B men and women left their homes in a panic
C there was fear that poisonous gas would be used
D men and women lost all faith in God
E some offered their help voluntarily to meet the disaster

19. In order to try to stop the panic caused by Orson Welles's programme which *three* of the following measures were taken?
    1. The broadcasting company's officials made careful statements.
    2. Reminders were given that this was a play.
    3. The police managed to restore order by patrolling.
    4. News bulletins explained fully what had happened.
    5. The public were told that it was a hoax.

A 1, 2, and 3 only
B 1, 2, and 4 only
C 1, 3, and 5 only
D 2, 4, and 5 only
E 3, 4, and 5 only

20. Which *two* of the following were direct results of the broadcast described in the passage?
    1. The radio company was censured.
    2. The public felt rather foolish.
    3. The producer's future improved.
    4. The state was very embarrassed.
    5. The dramatisations continued successfully.

A 1 and 2 only
B 1 and 3 only
C 2 and 4 only
D 3 and 5 only
E 4 and 5 only

Development

Further reading

1. H. G. Wells, *The War of the Worlds*, 1898, Penguin Books 1946.
2. A. C. Clarke, *Expedition to Earth*, 1954.
   This is a visit-by-aliens science fiction story with a difference which contains time-shifts. After man has destroyed his own world the Venusians visit the planet Earth and report back to their scientists that 'the most puzzling of the objects found . . . was a flat metal container holding a great length of transparent plastic material, perforated at the edges and wound tightly into a spool'. The pictures on the spool 'under the correct radiation . . . apparently form a record of life as it was on the Third Planet (Earth) at the height of its civilisation.' The discovery emerges as a Micky Mouse cartoon film!
   (This story is included in R. A. Banks (ed.), *Ten Science Fiction Stories*, Hodder and Stoughton, 1977.)

Written work

1. Imagine that a group of aliens visit this planet in the year 2050, after man has destroyed himself and his civilisation. Give an account of what they might find and what evidence they would discover about the kind of civilisation we built for ourselves; what would show our real values, our follies, our achievements seen through the eyes of alien visitors?
2. What advantages and disadvantages can you see in man's continued exploration of Space?

Dramatic activities

Take, as a group, a book you have enjoyed reading *or* a short story you know well *or* a newspaper article or feature. Then try to dramatise it to make it seem real and alive. (If you wish, you may like to produce it as a radio programme with the help of a cassette-recorder.)

Read the following passage very carefully; then answer the questions which follow. *DO NOT GUESS.*

The Dare

The tree was tremendous, an irate, steely black steeple beside the river. I was damned if I'd climb it. The hell with it! No one but Phineas could think up such a crazy idea.

He, of course, saw nothing the slightest bit intimidating about it. He wouldn't, or couldn't admit it if he did. Not Phineas.   5

'What I like best about this tree,' he said in that voice of his, the equivalence in sound of a hypnotist's eyes, 'what I like is that it's such a cinch!' He opened his green eyes wider and gave us his maniac look, and only the smirk on his wide mouth with its droll, slightly protruding upper lip gave us the reassurance that he wasn't completely goofy.   10

'Is that what you like best?' I said sarcastically. I said a lot of things sarcastically that summer; that was my sarcastic summer, 1942.

There were three others with us – Phineas in those days almost always moved in groups the size of a hockey team – and they stood with me looking with masked apprehension from him to the tree. Its soaring   15
black trunk was set with rough wooden pegs leading up to a substantial limb which extended further towards the water. Standing on this limb, you could by a prodigious effort jump far enough out into the river for safety. So we had heard. At least the seventeen-year-old bunch could do it.   20

We stood looking up at it, four looks of consternation, one of excitement. 'Do you want to go first?' Finny asked us rhetorically. We just looked quietly back at him; he was the one who was supposed to be the first to try. He began taking off his clothes, stripping down to his underpants.   25

He began scrambling clumsily up the wooden pegs nailed to the side of the tree, his back muscles working like a panther's. The pegs didn't seem strong enough to hold his weight. At last he stepped out onto the branch which reached a little further towards the water. 'Is this the one they jump from?' None of us knew. 'If I do it, you're all going to do it,   30
aren't you?' We didn't say anything very clearly. 'Well,' he cried out, 'here's my contribution to the war effort!' and he sprang out, fell through the tips of some lower branches and smashed into the water.

'Great!' he cried, bobbing instantly to the surface again, his wet hair plastered on his forehead. 'Who's next?'   35

I was. This tree flooded me with a sensation of alarm all the way to
my tingling fingers. My head began to feel unnaturally light, and the
vague rustling sounds from the nearby woods came to me as though
muffled and filtered. I took off my clothes and started to climb the pegs.
I don't remember saying anything. The branch he had jumped from   40
was slenderer than it looked from the ground and much higher. It was
impossible to walk out on it far enough to be well over the river. I
would have to spring far out or risk falling into the shallow water near
the bank. 'Come on,' drawled Finny from below, 'stop standing there
showing off. When they torpedo the troop ship,' he shouted, 'you can't   45
stand there admiring the view. Jump.'

'What was I doing up here anyway? Why did I let Finny talk me into
stupid things like this anyway?'

'Jump.'

With the sensation that I was throwing my life away, I jumped into   50
space. Some tips of branches slapped past me and then I crashed into
the water. My legs hit the soft mud of the bottom and immediately I
was on the surface again being congratulated. I felt fine.

'I think that was better than Finny's', said Elwin – better known as
Leper – Lepellier.   55

'All right, pal,' Finny spoke in his cordial, penetrating voice, that
reverberant instrument in his chest. 'Don't start awarding prizes until
you've passed the course. The tree is waiting.'

Leper closed his mouth as though forever. He didn't argue or refuse.
He didn't back away. He became inanimate. But the other two, Chet   60
Douglass and Bobby Zane, were vocal enough, complaining shrilly
about school regulations, the danger of stomach cramps, physical
disabilities they had never mentioned before.

'It's you, pal,' Finny said to me at last, 'just you and me!' We were
the best of friends at that moment.   65

1. Which one of the following is closest in meaning to 'irate' as used in
   line 1?
   A Huge
   B Mis-shapen
   C Angry
   D Awe-inspiring
   E Tall

2. The writer was damned if he'd climb the tree (line 2) because
   A he refused to be told what to do
   B Phineas was known to be rather mad
   C he was secretly very afraid of it
   D Phineas was always thinking up such ideas
   E he saw little point in tackling it

3. The comparison of Phineas's voice with 'a hypnotist's eyes (lines 6–7) is intended to emphasise that it
   A could not be disregarded
   B was full of menace
   C was not at all rational
   D sent everyone into a trance
   E could not be understood clearly

4. Which one of the following expressions is closest in meaning to 'it's such a cinch!' as used in lines 7–8?
   A It's a slice of luck!
   B It's a real challenge!
   C It's a chance in a million!
   D It's a bit of a lark!
   E It's a piece of cake!

5. Judging from lines 1–10, Phineas was
   A mad
   B daring
   C selfish
   D boastful
   E spiteful

6. The word 'sarcastically' (line 11) suggests mainly that the writer spoke in a tone of voice which was
   A casual
   B sneering
   C serious
   D questioning
   E hesitant

7. The writer's sarcastic remark (line 11) was essentially unfair because
   A he had misunderstood what Phineas had said
   B what Phineas had said irritated him a lot
   C he had not heard what Phineas had said
   D what Phineas had said made little sense
   E he had misquoted what Phineas had said

8. Which one of the following words is closest in meaning to 'prodigious' as used in line 18?
   A Magnificent
   B Gigantic
   C Miraculous
   D Determined
   E Maximum

9. It was important to 'jump far enough out into the river' (line 18) in order to
   A reach the opposite bank
   B show off to everyone
   C make an enormous splash
   D fall into deeper water
   E get clear of the branch

10. When Finny asked 'Do you want to go first?' (line 22) it was obvious from his voice that he
    A thought the others were cowards
    B did not want to jump
    C had begun to sneer openly
    D did not expect an answer
    E wondered if he could succeed

11. The reason nobody replied to Finny's question 'Do you want to go first?' (line 10) was that
    A everyone wanted to see what would happen
    B he was hoping to wriggle out of it
    C it had been agreed it should be him
    D he was daring everyone to challenge him
    E everyone knew it was far too dangerous

12. The way Finny climbed the tree could be described as being all the following *EXCEPT*
    A struggling
    B energetic
    C nervous
    D awkward
    E determined

13. The reason why the rest 'didn't say anything very clearly' (line 31) when Finny spoke to them was that they
    A were totally lost for words to reply
    B knew their bluff had finally been called
    C hoped he would call the thing off
    D wondered if they could do it themselves
    E refused to be bullied into doing anything

14. As the writer prepared himself and climbed the tree he felt particularly
    A giddy
    B terrified
    C empty
    D stupid
    E confused

15. Which *three* things surprised the writer about the branch when he reached it? He had expected it to be
    1. longer
    2. harder
    3. thicker
    4. barer
    5. lower

    A 1, 2, and 3 only
    B 1, 2, and 4 only
    C 1, 3, and 5 only
    D 2, 4, and 5 only
    E 3, 4, and 5 only

16. Finny's remarks to the writer as he hesitated before jumping (lines 44–46) were really
    A taunts
    B applause
    C jokes
    D encouragement
    E boasts

17. The two questions in inverted commas (lines 47–48) represent
    A answers to Finny's shouts
    B the writer's innermost thoughts
    C things the writer asked Finny
    D the writer's comments to others
    E excuses the writer was making

18. The jumps made by Finny and the writer were identical in all the following respects *EXCEPT* that both boys
    A leapt out off the branch
    B hit branches on the way down
    C fell heavily into the water
    D rose at once to the surface
    E received congratulations from the boys

19. The word 'cordial' (line 56) is probably used by the writer
    A sarcastically
    B frankly
    C literally
    D bitterly
    E figuratively

20. The effect of Finny's remarks (lines 56–58) on Chet Douglass and Bobby Zane was to make them

A feel ill
B offer excuses
C obey regulations
D run away
E nervous

Development

Further reading

1. R. M. Ballantyne, *The Coral Island*, 1856.
   A story of adventure. A group of boys find themselves shipwrecked amongst some coral islands in the Pacific Ocean. They work and play happily together in the paradise they have found until they are rescued.
2. William Golding, *Lord of the Flies*, Faber and Faber, 1954.
   This is also a story of adventure. A group of boys find themselves, without any adults, on an island after their plane has crashed. They gradually find that the wickedness of human beings lies just beneath the surface as they live and fight and kill each other until they are rescued.

Written work

1. Write a short story entitled *The Dare*. Make sure that the topic is central to the story you give. Try to build up your narrative to reach a climax at the end.
2. Give an account of one or two occasions when you have been dared to do something which you knew was dangerous or wrong. Explain why you felt you had to agree to take the dare or to refuse it. What finally happened?
3. Find the life story of a famous man or woman who accepted the challenge to undertake something that was dangerous or difficult for a cause he or she believed in. Summarise his or her life story in about 250 words. (*A few suggestions*: Sir Thomas More; Martin Luther; St Joan; Mother Teresa; Martin Luther King.)
   If you wish, you may give an account, instead, of a group of people who have 'dared' to pursue a cause they believed was right. (*A few suggestions*: The Tolpuddle Martyrs; The Suffragettes; The Pilgrim Fathers; The Greenham Common Peace Women.)

Read the following passage very carefully; then answer the questions which
follow. *DO NOT GUESS.*

The Plague

Rats were only indirectly responsible for the Plague; the real culprits
for the spread of the disease were the infected fleas which lived
parasitically on the rats; they transferred the illness to human beings
and from one person to another. Moreover, the Plague was not a single
disease with only one form; there were at least three kinds; the common   5
form, or *bubonic*, which caused swellings in the groins and armpits and
black patches on the skin and usually killed patients in about a week;
the *pneumonic*, which attacked the lungs, caused haemorrhages, was
highly contagious, and killed patients in about three days; the third
form, the *septicaemic*, was the most dangerous, virulent, and swift-   10
acting, since it attacked the bloodstream and killed within hours rather
than days. The infection carried by fleas from the body of a sick or
dying person became effectively an inoculation of death itself.
    The Plague spread from the coasts and attacked large cities and
small villages alike; there were few who fell sick who kept their beds for   15
more than three days, although some unfortunate ones found their rest
only after a week. In one small village more than 380 died, most of the
parish. In the same year (1349) there was an epidemic amongst sheep
everywhere; their disease resembled man's but it was not the same.
Prices of goods fell sharply for few were rash enough to carry much   20
money about them, lest they fell sick and were robbed. It was a
common sight to see cattle lying in ditches into which they had fallen
and died, since there were no longer enough farm-hands to mend the
fences and look after the animals. Churches were so poor that they
could not maintain their offices, although many illiterate men took holy   25
orders once their wives had died of the pestilence. It was sad to see
great and small buildings falling into ruins without repair; villages were
wiped out or deserted as their populations fell foul of the Plague or fled.
    When the Plague attacked a community it ran riot with the speed of
wildfire, from town to town and from village to village. Parsons   30
announced to their congregations the arrival of the disease in
neighbouring parishes with fear and trembling; pedlars stumbled from
plague-stricken areas into communities which immediately barred
their doors and shut tight their windows. Sanitary conditions were bad,
both primitive and scarce. The disposal of rubbish and sewage posed   35
enormous problems for those trying to contain the disease, since with

the filth came the rats, in even larger numbers, and with the rats the fleas, and with the fleas, the Plague. In London most of the rubbish found its way into the Thames and there the burial of the dead became such a major problem that many bodies were left unburied, although 40 they were placed in guarded or prohibited areas. Criminals flocked to the towns to plunder abandoned churches and to loot deserted houses standing vulnerable and deserted.

About a third of the nation's population probably died at this time. Labour was scarce, therefore, and those who survived could ask for 45 higher wages. The economy of England had been in decline well before 1349, however, and the slump was not caused by the Plague. A noticeable feature of the labour market was that men and their families moved about more easily in search of employment. Work was more available throughout the country. One wonders, nevertheless, just how 50 many artists and writers, craftsmen and architects, wood-carvers and glassworkers perished in just two years. We shall never know; but the nation was impoverished by the Plague.

1. The first sentence ('Rats . . . another'; lines 1–4) suggests that
   A rats had no part in the spread of the Plague
   B fleas infected the rats on whom they lived
   C rats carried the Plague which was transmitted to man by fleas
   D rats incubated the Plague without suffering any harm themselves
   E rats suffered by being constantly re-infected by parasitic fleas

2. The first sentence (lines 1–4) also suggests that the Plague was spread directly in which *two* of the following ways?
   1. From rat to flea
   2. From flea to human being
   3. From one human to another
   4. From rat to human being
   5. From flea to rat

   A 1 and 2 only
   B 1 and 5 only
   C 2 and 3 only
   D 3 and 4 only
   E 4 and 5 only

3. Which *two* of the following symptoms marked the form of the Plague most frequently found?
   1. Lumps in the glands
   2. Severe loss of blood
   3. Discoloured patches on the skin
   4. Sudden fever causing death
   5. Poisoning of the blood

A 1 and 2 only
B 1 and 3 only
C 2 and 4 only
D 3 and 5 only
E 4 and 5 only

4. Which one of the following is closest in meaning to 'virulent' as used in
   line 10?
   A Highly lethal
   B Most painful
   C Highly malignant
   D Most distressing
   E Highly infectious

5. The form of the Plague which killed its victims the fastest did so by
   attacking the
   A skin
   B glands
   C heart
   D lungs
   E blood

6. Which one of the following words is closest in meaning to 'effectively' as
   used in line 13?
   A Inevitably
   B Deliberately
   C Actually
   D Scientifically
   E Eventually

7. 'There were few who fell sick who kept their beds for more than three
   days' (lines 15–16) means that there were few who
   A recovered from the disease
   B avoided being infected by others
   C died in a few days
   D survived for very long
   E were struck down at once

8. The ones who 'found their rest only after a week' (lines 16–17) are
   described as *unfortunate* because
   A they suffered for much longer
   B their hopes were dashed
   C they died in the end
   D their illness produced lumps
   E they had seemed to recover

9. 'Prices of goods fell sharply' (line 20) because
   A people were too ill to do shopping
   B money was very difficult to earn
   C death led to much lower demand
   D money was kept out of circulation
   E people preferred to stay safely at home

10. Cattle fell into ditches and died (lines 22–23) because
    A they fell sick with plague-like illnesses
    B there were few people to care for them
    C they pleased themselves what they did
    D there was a breakdown in law and order
    E they took advantage of their new-found freedom

11. Which one of the following is closest in meaning to 'offices' as used in line 26?
    A Charitable works
    B Services
    C Ecclesiastical buildings
    D Regulations
    E Administrative affairs

12. Which one of the following words is closest in meaning to 'illiterate' as used in line 25?
    A Unintelligent
    B Irreligious
    C Uneducated
    D Inappropriate
    E Uncivilised

13. All the following were the direct effects of the Plague *EXCEPT*
    A the decay of farms
    B an increase in violence
    C the destruction of communities
    D a decrease in trade
    E the deterioration of property

14. The poor sanitary conditions were made worse by all the following *EXCEPT*
    A the difficulty of waste-disposal
    B corpses collected but left unburied
    C the pollution of major rivers
    D robbers vandalising buildings left unoccupied
    E the increase of the rat-population

15. Which one of the following is closest in meaning to 'vulnerable' as used in line 43?

A Open to attack
B Asking for trouble
C In bad condition
D Abandoned by everyone
E Waiting for vandals

16. The effects of the huge death-toll on the labour market included all the following *EXCEPT*
    A better wages on demand
    B a more mobile work-force
    C more jobs available everywhere
    D a reduction in skilled men
    E better chances of promotion

17. Which one of the following is closest in meaning to 'impoverished' as used in line 53?
    A Overwhelmed
    B Made weaker
    C Exhausted
    D Made poorer
    E Depleted

18. According to the passage as a whole, all the following were prominent features of the Plague *EXCEPT*
    A the increase in robbery it brought
    B the speed with which it killed
    C the strength with which it attacked
    D the speed with which it spread
    E the loss of faith it caused

19. The passage deals with the effect of the Plague on all the following areas of life *EXCEPT*
    A economics
    B medicine
    C crime
    D farming
    E religion

20. If you had suffered from the Plague in 1349, it was certain that at least one of the following facts would have applied to you *EXCEPT* that you had
    A been bitten by a flea from an infected person
    B touched the body of a farm animal which had died mysteriously
    C been in recent contact with a carrier of the disease
    D lived in conditions which encouraged the growth of vermin
    E been bitten by a flea from an infected rat

Development

Further reading

1. Philip Ziegler, *The Black Death*, Penguin, 1969.
2. Daniel Defoe, *A Journal of the Plague Year*, first published in 1722, Penguin English Library, 1966.

   This claims to be an account of the year of the Great Plague 1664–1665, in London written by an eye-witness. It is full of the most graphic details, such as the carts for the dead rolling through the streets, the effect on trade, and the burial of the victims in huge pits. This plague infestation was an attack of bubonic plague.

Written work

1. Write five entries for a personal journal which set out your experiences as someone caught up in an outbreak of an incurable disease in your area.
2. Describe what you consider to be the biggest threat to your safety today. Explain how you think the danger can be averted.

Further activities

1. Investigate and write a report on the work of *one* of the following, who made a major contribution to new discoveries in medical science:

   e.g. William Harvey; Edward Jenner; Sir Alexander Fleming.
2. Find out as much as you can about the aims and activities of a charity dedicated to discovering the causes of a disease which is so far impossible or difficult to cure:

   e.g. Multiple Scelerosis Society of Great Britain and Northern Ireland; The Leukaemia Research Fund; The Imperial Cancer Research Fund.

Exploration 20

Read the following passage very carefully; then answer the questions which follow. *DO NOT GUESS.*

The Jungle

At twilight there is usually an uncanny hush in the jungle, just before the evening chorus of crickets, cicadas, and other insects starts up. It was deadly still, when suddenly a tall palm frond started swinging madly backwards and forwards for no apparent reason. For some time I had had the uneasy feeling that I was being followed. I heard a   5
stealthy sound behind me, but when I stopped to listen the rustling stopped too. I was sure it was a tiger. I could feel the hair standing up on the back of my neck. Suddenly a stick snapped. I wanted to run, but after all I had a gun. Anyway, it was no good running. I might bump into a Jap patrol or a party of aborigines with their blow-pipes and   10
poisoned darts. I should not be able to watch the track carefully and put my foot on a snake or a scorpion – an obscene creature with shining black claws and poisonous sting waving in the air. But I got back to camp all right, just as night fell.

A year or two later, how different the jungle seemed! But the change   15
was in me, not in the jungle. By this time I knew the aborigines; I knew that the last thing they would want to do would be to shoot a poisoned dart at me or anyone else. I was not afraid of running into a Jap patrol, because experience had taught me that they travelled so noisily and that their reactions were so slow that one could just step off the path   20
and hide till they passed. Snakes, centipedes, and scorpions of the dimensions of tea-plates I was no longer afraid of, for in those years I had not heard of a single aborigine or Chinese, most of them going barefoot as I did, being bitten by a snake except for one pulling up tapioca by the roots – and he had not died.   25

1. Which one of the following is closest in meaning to 'uncanny' as it is used in line 1?
   A Dramatic
   B Baffling
   C Weird
   D Supernatural
   E Abnormal

2. The first sentence (lines 1–2) suggests that just before 'the evening chorus' the jungle is all the following *EXCEPT*

A quite silent
B growing dark
C strange in atmosphere
D behaving naturally
E totally deserted

3. In the expression, 'It was deadly still' (lines 2–3), *It* refers to the
   A twilight
   B hush
   C jungle
   D evening
   E chorus

4. In the first two sentences ('At twilight . . . reason') in (lines 1–4) all the following words help to stress that the writer was feeling uneasy *EXCEPT*
   A 'usually' (line 1)
   B 'uncanny' (line 1)
   C 'deadly' (line 3)
   D 'suddenly' (line 3)
   E 'madly' (line 4)

5. The sudden 'swinging madly backwards and forwards' of the palm frond (lines 3–4) worried the writer for which *two* of the following reasons?
   1. The hush in the jungle was quite abnormal.
   2. He had already felt he was being followed.
   3. There was no immediate explanation for it.
   4. He had heard noises behind him earlier on.
   5. The insects seemed to know there was danger.

   A 1 and 2 only
   B 1 and 4 only
   C 2 and 3 only
   D 3 and 5 only
   E 4 and 5 only

6. The word 'stealthy', as it is used in line 6, suggests that the writer felt that his pursuer was being all the following *EXCEPT* very careful to
   A remain out of sight
   B keep close on his track
   C make very little noise
   D watch his movements very closely
   E frighten him into making mistakes

7. All the following led the writer to the conclusion, 'I was sure it was a tiger' (line 7) *EXCEPT*

   A a sudden movement among the leaves
   B the feeling he was being stalked
   C a furtive sound behind him
   D the silence when he stopped
   E a noise of a breaking twig

8. The word 'but' in line 13 helps to stress the fact that
   A the writer did not in fact run away
   B a tiger was no match for a gun
   C the writer was ashamed of his cowardice
   D a gun would have slowed him down
   E the writer felt too paralysed to run far

9. The *three* reasons why the writer felt 'it was no good running' (line 9)
   were that
      1. there were advantages in facing an enemy
      2. the tiger would surely catch him
      3. there were enemy forces close by
      4. the natives might strike him down
      5. there were poisonous creatures in his path

   A 1, 2, and 3 only
   B 1, 2, and 5 only
   C 1, 3, and 4 only
   D 2, 4, and 5 only
   E 3, 4, and 5 only

10. Which one of the following is closest in meaning to 'obscene' as it is used
    in line 12?
    A Filthy
    B Disgusting
    C Dangerous
    D Deceptive
    E Evil

11. The jungle seems so different 'a year or two later' (line 15) because
    A the war had come to an end
    B time had mellowed his earlier memories
    C the aborigines had become more peaceful
    D time had reduced the dangers all around
    E the author had a lot more knowledge

12. From the passage all the following are true of 'the aborigines' (line 16)
    EXCEPT that they
    A lay in wait for travellers
    B used home-made improvised weapons
    C had a fearsome but false reputation
    D were normally peaceful people
    E lived in the jungle

13. As the writer got to know the aborigines better he discovered that they
    were
    A retiring
    B primitive
    C friendly
    D elusive
    E loyal

14. The writer was no longer 'afraid of running into a Jap patrol' (line 18)
    because
    A he knew the aborigines would protect him
    B enemy soldiers lacked skill in jungle warfare
    C he had learnt more about his enemy
    D enemy failed to understand jungle conditions
    E he realised noises travelled in the jungle

15. For which *two* of the following reasons could the writer avoid Jap
    patrols?
        1. They moved in large groups.
        2. They announced their presence loudly.
        3. They were afraid of the aborigines.
        4. They failed to respond quickly.
        5. They kept only to recognised paths.

    A 1 and 3 only
    B 1 and 5 only
    C 2 and 3 only
    D 2 and 4 only
    E 4 and 5 only

16. The comparison of the scorpions with 'tea-plates' (line 22) is intended
    to emphasise their
    A colour
    B hardness
    C flatness
    D roundness
    E size

17. The reason why the writer was no longer afraid of snakes, centipedes,
    and scorpions (lines 21–22) was that
    A the inhabitants of the jungle went barefoot
    B he realised mortal bites were very rare
    C the jungle provided him with considerable cover
    D he recognised the real danger was the enemy
    E the size of the creatures gave them away

18. The writer mentions that the man bitten by the snake had been 'pulling up tapioca by the roots' (lines 24–25) in order to suggest mainly that
    A it was his own fault through going barefoot
    B snakes attacked only when they were attacked
    C such events occurred only in cultivated land
    D snakes lived only among plants of this kind
    E it was likely he had disturbed a snake's lair

19. The second paragraph differs from the first mainly in the way it
    A explains that the jungle was quite safe
    B shows the writer's contempt for his enemy
    C emphasises the writer's increased confidence and experience
    D shows that jungle life was really attractive
    E expresses the writer's admiration of the aborigines

20. The passage as a whole includes comments by the writer on all the following *EXCEPT* his
    A principles
    B ignorance
    C fears
    D experience
    E observations

Development

Further reading

1. F. Spencer Chapman, *Living Dangerously*, The Queen's Classics, Chatto and Windus, 1953.
   The Jungle is Neutral, Chatto and Windus, 1949.
   Both these books are by the author of the passage used in this exercise; they are full of excitement and adventure.
2. J. H. Williams, *Elephant Bill*, Penguin Books, 1982.
   This is a gripping account of the way elephants and man lived, helping each other, and died together in the jungles of Burma particularly during The Second World War; the author describes them as 'the most lovable and sagacious of all beasts'.

Written work

1. An account of an exciting adventure which happened to you, written as part of your longer autobiography.
2. Write two paragraphs for your personal diary; the first should give an account of a place you visited for the first time two or three years ago; the second should be an account of your visit to the same place made a few weeks ago.

Talking and activities

1. Visit a library to find out as much as you can about the hardships suffered by people in the jungle during The Second World War. Prepare a talk to give to your class about the subject.
2. Arrange a class discussion (or a more formal debate) on the theme: 'We must take more care to preserve the jungles of the world.' (Remember that many of the tropical rain-forests of South America are under serious threat today and their loss would affect not only the ecology of the area but also the weather world-wide.) What points would you like to emphasise?

Answers and keys

Part One

Exercise 1

1. Can you understand what you are reading?
2. It's easy but it takes some sorting out.
3. Words whose letters are jumbled together are called anagrams.
4. But they are anagrams only if they make new words.
5. Crosswords or Scrabble are much more fun.
6. Sometimes you can guess the words at once.
7. At other times you have to work them out.
8. Simple codes can be made up using letters.
9. Codes used by spies are much more complicated.
10. You need to be a good speller for this exercise.

Exercise 2

1. Interesting games are sometimes played with the help of computers.
2. They often involve chasing and destroying an enemy.
3. I wonder why they are always so violent.
4. It must be the killer instinct coming out.
5. Not all men and women want to destroy things. (There are more sinister orders possible here!)
6. What would you like to see about the games?
7. Perhaps bringing help to those in need is not so dramatic.
8. A relief mission to help earthquake victims could be exciting.
9. Give me every time the interception and destruction of invaders from outer space!
10. Why not invent a computer game based on athletics or some other sport?

Exercise 3

1. There were no curtains up. (Barry Hines, *Kes*)
2. A certain man had two sons. (The parable of *The Prodigal Son*)
3. Once upon a time there were three bears. (A fairy story: *Goldilocks and the Three Bears*)
4. He was an old man who fished alone. (E. Hemingway, *The Old Man and the Sea*)
5. On Friday, 12th June, I woke up at six o'clock and no wonder; it was my birthday. (*The Diary of Anne Frank*)
6. A tortoise and a hare started to dispute which was the swifter. (Æsop's fable, *The Tortoise and the Hare*)
7. One thing that was certain, the white kitten had had nothing to do with it. (Lewis Carroll, *Alice through the Looking Glass*)
8. My father had a small estate in Nottinghamshire; I was the third of five sons. (J. Swift, *Gulliver's Travels*)

9. I was born in the year 1632 in the city of York. (Daniel Defoe, *Robinson Crusoe*)
10. This book is largely concerned with Hobbits. (J. R. R. Tolkien, Prologue to *The Lord of the Rings*)

Exercise 4

1. (a), (c), (d), (b).
2. (e), (b), (d), (c), (a).
3. (b), (e), (d), (a), (c), (f).
4. (c), (a), (e), (b), (e).
5. (b), (d), (c), (e), (a).
6. (e), (b), (a), (d), (c).
7. (d), (a), (b), (e), (c), (f).
8. (d), (b), (e), (c), (a).
9. (a), (d), (c), (b).
10. (e), (d), (c), (a), (b), (f).

Exercise 5

Correct order: lines 1, 3, 2, 8, 4, 6, 5, 7.

Exercise 6

Suggested correct order: 1, 4, 2, 7, 5, 8, 3, 6, 9, 10.

Exercise 8

I bought . . . . He came home . . . . What's happened . . . . I'm not Liverpool . . . . Why not? . . . . Because Harold Bullock . . . . To be absolutely honest . . . . A couple of months ago . . . . Which ones are Leeds United? . . . . Neither . . . . Oh! . . . . As far as I could gather . . . . .

Exercise 9

(*a*) 1. *carry* 2. *spots* 3. *cruelty* 4. *follow* 5. *nature reserves.*
(*b*) 1. *experience* 2. *fast* 3. *feared (expected)* 4. *explanation* 5. *enclosure (pen, fold)* 6. *minority* 7. *loudly* 8. *traditional* 9. *responded (answered)* 10. *expected.*
(*c*) (i) *I heard a noise* . . . . *I head it again (it came again)* . . . . *I got up* . . . . *went into the corridor* . . . . *I rushed in* . . . . *he was dead.*

(adapted from Charlotte Brontë, *Jane Eyre*)

(ii) *a little girl to come along carrying a basket of food* . . . . *where she was going* . . . . *went away (left her)* . . . . *the wolf did not look like her grandmother* . . . . *shot the wolf.*

(Based on James Thurber, *Fables for our Time*)

Exercise 10

5, 3, 6, 1, 9, 2, 4, 8, 7.

Exercises *11, 12, 13, 14, 15*

(T = True; F = False)

Exercise	Question			
	1 2 3 4 5	6 7 8 9 10	11 12 13 14 15	16 17 18 19 20
11	T T T F F	F T T F F	F T F T F	T T F T T
12	T F F T F	T F T T F	T F T T F	T T F F F
13	T F T F F	T F T T F	F F T F F	F T T F F
14	F T T F T	F F T F T	T T F T F	F T T T F
15	F T F T F	F T T F F	F T T F T	T T F F F

Chapter *3*

Page oo (a) Key is C (A poon).
Page oo (b) Key is D (Cats and Dogs).
Page oo (iv) Key is A (Kneesup).

Exercise *16*

1. 1945 2. Invent your own key 3. Rugby 4. Pony-riding 5. Invent your own key 6. (NB section): 'Every cloud has a silver lining'; 'It's the last straw that breaks the camel's back'. 7. *e.g.* CVO, FCO, GPO, GSO, ISO, MVO, NCO, POO, PRO, RCO, RLO etc. 8. *Delinquent* (given in Brewer's *Dictionary of Phrase and Fable*) 9. *Demonstrating* was the word used in the article, but *Protesting* would be correct too. 10. Invent your own key.

Exercise *17*

9. *e.g.* Cove, Fellow, Creature, Mate, etc.
10. *e.g.* a biography, an advertisement, a short story, a diary, a newspaper article, an obituary, a White Paper, a newspaper.

Part Two

(T = True; F = False)

Exploration		1	2	3	4	5	6	7	8	9	10	11	12	13	14	15	16	17	18	19	20	21	22	23	24	25
1.	I Map-reading	D	D	B	D	E	–	–	–	–	–						–	–	–	–	–	–	–			
	II The Highway Code	–	–	–	–	–	B	C	A	C	B	T	F	–	–	–	D	D	C	D	A	–	–			
2.	A home computer I	T	F	F	F	T	T	T	F	F	T	A	A	B	B	C	B	A	B	A	A	–	–			
	II	C	B	B	C	A	C	B	D	D	C	D	C	B	D	A	C	B	B	B	D	–	–			
3.	Strange pets	A	C	A	A	C	A	B	A	A	A	D	A	C	B	C	A	A	A	C	A	–	–			
4.	The wedding	C	A	B	A	D	B	C	D	C	B	D	C	C	B	A	C	B	B	B	D	–	–			
5.	A taste of France	D	B	C	A	C	A	B	D	C	A	B	D	D	B	D	B	B	C	B	C	B	C			
6.	The Hindenberg	C	A	B	B	D	B	B	D	A	D	C	C	A	C	A	C	C	A	A	D	–	–			
7.	Floods in Florence	A	A	A	D	B	B	D	D	D	B	D	D	D	C	C	A	B	A	C	A	–	C			
8.	Robots	B	B	E	E	E	E	C	D	B	E	B	D	D	B	C	D	E	E	D	A	A	C	B	D	E
9.	A little sister's nightmare	B	A	C	C	A	B	E	A	E	D	C	E	E	C	D	D	B	C	E	B	–	–			
10.	The rattlesnake	E	A	C	C	B	B	B	B	E	A	B	D	C	C	B	B	E	C	A	C	–	–			
11.	Grabbing your attention	D	D	C	A	C	B	D	A	C	A	A	A	E	B	A	C	E	C	A	C	–	–			
12.	St. Anthony's Fire	D	E	A	C	C	E	A	B	E	C	A	D	B	D	E	E	B	B	A	D	–	–			
13.	The new teacher	C	C	C	B	C	B	E	A	B	A	B	C	C	B	C	C	C	C	C	E	–	–			
14.	The school record	C	A	E	D	B	E	B	D	D	A	A	B	C	B	A	A	A	C	C	B	–	–			
15.	Running away	D	A	E	D	E	B	B	E	E	C	E	C	B	B	E	D	B	C	C	C	–	–			
16.	The motor-bike	D	E	C	C	B	C	D	D	E	E	E	D	B	E	A	A	C	A	B	B	–	–			
17.	U.F.O.s	A	E	B	D	B	A	B	D	B	E	C	C	C	B	E	D	C	D	B	B	–	–			
18.	The dare	C	C	A	E	B	B	E	D	D	D	C	C	C	B	C	C	B	D	A	B	–	–			
19.	The plague	C	A	B	C	E	D	D	A	D	B	B	B	D	D	A	E	B	E	B	B	–	–			
20.	The jungle	C	E	C	A	C	E	E	A	E	B	E	A	C	C	D	B	B	E	C	A	–	–			